TWO LADIES OF COLONIAL ALGERIA

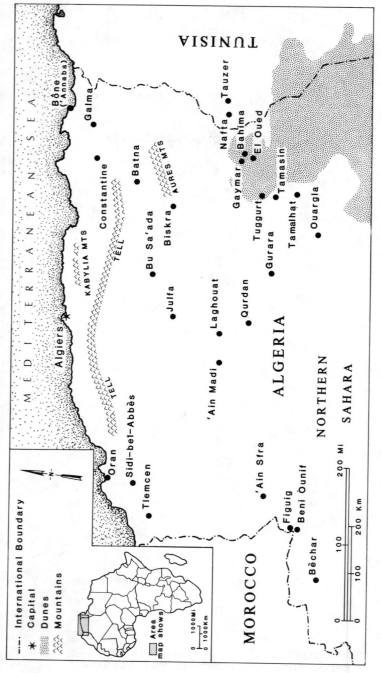

Location Map of Northern Algeria

TWO LADIES OF COLONIAL ALGERIA

THE LIVES AND TIMES OF AURÉLIE PICARD

AND

ISABELLE EBERHARDT

by

Ursula Kingsmill Hart

Ohio University Center for International Studies
Monographs in International Studies

African Series Number 49
Athens, Ohio   1987

Library of Congress Cataloging-in-Publication Data

Hart, Ursula Kingsmill.
    Two ladies of colonial Algeria.

    (Monographs in international studies. African
series ; no. 49)
        Bibliography: p.
        1. Picard, Aurelie, 1849–1933.   2. Eberhardt,
Isabelle, 1877–1904.   3. Algeria—Biography.
4. Tijaniyah—Algeria—History.   5. Women—Biography.
I. Title.   II. Series.
DT294.7.A1H37   1987   965'009'92 [B]   87-11094
ISBN 0-89680-143-8

ISBN 0-89680-143-8

DEDICATION

To Dave, who was so often dragged away from his own work, though not necessarily uncomplainingly, to sort out my garbled manuscript and even more muddled footnotes, with all my love.

URSULA KINGSMILL HART was born in India of British parents. She was educated in the French Lycee system and grew up in Morocco, where she eventually met her anthropologist husband, David Montgomery Hart. The Harts live in the Almeria province of Southeastern Spain.

CONTENTS

ILLUSTRATIONS

FOREWORD

This study has been a decade in gestation. It was originally suggested to me on our original visit to the French Algerian Archives (Archives d'Outre-Mer) at Aix-en-Provence by the Deputy Archivist (Sous-Archiviste) there, Dr. Charles Uthéza who thought that a comparison of the careers of Aurélie Picard and Isabelle Eberhardt might prove profitable. As I agreed fully, I decided to pursue it, and my most heartfelt thanks are due to Dr. Uthéza for having made the suggestion in the first place, and also to his erstwhile superior, Dr. Pierre Boyer, the then director of the archives. My husband and I spent two exploratory weeks there in the fall of 1974 and then put in over two months of hard work there during a disastrously wet season on a camping site in the fall of 1976.

Apart from the foregoing individuals, my thanks are also due to Dr. Donald C. Holsinger, who made a special trip out of his way in order to obtain photographs of the one-time Aurélie Picard-Sidi Ahmad Tijani farm and residence at Qurdan, in South-Central Algeria; to Miss Carmen Muñoz for the drawings; to Miss Clare Usher for having done the tedious job of typing the final draft; to my daughter, Mrs. Carrol Johnson, who was the guineapig reader of the first draft and whose constructive criticism and suggestions were so encouraging; and, last but not least, to my husband David M. Hart. Much of the work in this book is his, and I acknowledge this fact with affection and with love.

These two charming vignettes offer fascinating and unusual insights into networks of human relationships seldom portrayed in the context of colonial Algeria. Both Aurélie Picard and Isabelle Eberhardt married Algerian Muslims and through their husbands interacted with North African Muslim society in ways rarely experienced by their European contemporaries.

This study is particularly valuable for the light it sheds on successive leaders of the Tijaniya tariqa, a Sufi religious order more closely linked to French interests and policies than perhaps any other in colonial Algeria. Through her marriage to two successive leaders of the order, Aurélie Picard Tijani promoted the cause of France for more than six decades during the zenith of the colonial era. The author has effectively drawn on the abundant archival sources in Aix-en-Provence to develop a well-rounded portrait of Mme Tijani.

Isabelle Eberhardt Ehnni, of Russian and German origins, played a far different role. Drawn to North Africa at a young age, she readily accepted Islam, identified herself with Algerian Muslim society, and became far more critical of French policies and hence more threatening to French authorities than Mme Tijani. Though her husband had gained French citizenship because of his military service as a non-commissioned officer or spahi, his social prestige ranked far below that of the Tijani brothers.

The ultimate value of this work lies in its effective portrayal of two remarkably energetic, determined, and eccentric human beings. Though one became a Muslim while the other apparently adhered steadfastly to her Christian faith, both had to overcome the obstacles which face outsiders seeking acceptance in a community not their own. In their adamant refusal to conform to the norm of behavior in a colonial situation, they forged complex and tangled relationships with both colonizers and colonized which may surprise the reader but which also portended the ultimate failure of the French in Algeria.

Gifford B. Doxsee
Ohio University

INTRODUCTION

Although the lives of Aurélie Picard Tijani and Isabelle Eberhardt provide only a sidelight on the total historical canvas of French domination of Algeria, these Frenchwomen are noteworthy in that they married Algerian Muslims. The considerable differences between Picard and Eberhardt and their husbands illuminates the vast range of French and Algerian responses to conditions during the late nineteenth and early twentieth centuries.

Aurélie Picard was a prim and eminently respectable lower middle-class girl from Champagne who married the shaikh, or local head, of a Muslim religious order, the Tijaniya. This order was influential in both Morocco and Algeria but was much less supportive of France in Morocco. Thus Picard became both a pillar of and a thorn in the side of the French colonial establishment. On the whole, she always identified with France and French interests, policies and objectives.

Isabelle Eberhardt, on the other hand, was wayward, tomboyish, and nonconformist. Not even French in origin but White Russian, and of a semi-aristocratic parentage in circumstances of genteel poverty, she nonetheless spent her formative years in French-speaking Switzerland and then went to Algeria, discovered Islam, and became totally devoted to her conception of the Islamic way of life. She consorted and caroused with French army and foreign legion personnel and then caused a scandal by marrying a humble and not overly bright Algerian spahi or cavalry corporal, named Sliman Ehnni (probably properly Ahanni). Although dissolute, she nonetheless had certain literary pretensions and even left some published work behind after her tragic death in a Saharan flash flood in 1904 at the age of twenty-seven. Her identification was totally with Islam, at least in its local Algerian manifestations. Indeed, a case can be made that she was both a mystic and minor forerunner of modern Algerian nationalism.

There is no evidence that Picard and Eberhardt

knew each other personally, but they certainly must have heard of each other and equally certainly, neither one would have liked what she heard about the other. The mass of archival material on Picard which is available for consultation at Aix-en-Provence, contrasts with the scanty holdings concerning Eberhardt in the same archive, and this fact seems an accurate gauge as to how each was regarded by the colonial administration. Although in the last analysis it is to Eberhardt and not to Picard that one's sympathies must extend, Picard with her manipulations and full-scale participation in the internal politics of the Tijaniya order is nonetheless the more interesting of the two.

PART ONE: AURÉLIE PICARD

Chapter 1

THE COLONIAL ALGERIAN SCENE (1830-1871) AND
THE RISE OF THE TIJANIYA ORDER (1781-1820)

There is no question but that the French
conquest begun in 1830 was the most devastating
event in the history of nineteenth century Algeria.
At the time, the conquest was seen as a French
retaliation against Husain Dey, the last Ottoman
Turkish ruler, who had struck a French consul in the
face with a fly-whisk three years previously. The
French quickly and unceremoniously put an end to
three centuries of Ottoman occupation and
administration (which had been both more just and
efficient than has generally been supposed).[1]
      This introductory chapter can only provide the
most fleeting possible resumé of the first forty
years of French Algeria, followed by a further
summary account of the rise of the Tijaniya order.
The canvas of this book is small but that of its
total Algerian backdrop is vast, and therefore some
allusion to this vastness cannot be avoided.
      Physically, Algeria is vast: there are 90,000
square miles of it. Four times the size of France,
it takes at least three full days of modern travel
to drive from the Moroccan border in the northwest
to the Tunisian border in the northeast, while the
north-south distance from Algiers to the Ahaggar
mountains in the south-central Sahara is over twice
this, no less than 1,300 miles. Although the action
of the story takes place only on the northern edge
of the Sahara, fully four-fifths of the country is
desert. Today this is its economic underbelly,
piping out natural gas through SONATRACH auspices to
Mediterranean ports. Only the populous northern
tier, known as the Tell, has the orchards and the
vineyards of the Oranie, the jagged peaks of Kabylia
and the Jurjura, the Kansas-like upland wheatfields
of the Constantinois and the three major cities of
Oran, Algiers and Constantine. The population of
the Ottoman Regency in 1830 (which extended only to
the southern limits of the Tell) is estimated at

3

three million, while Algeria's current population (total land area) is approximately twenty million.

As all observers have noted, the French conquest of Algeria was neither an instantaneous nor a single-blanket operation, hardly possible at the time in a country of this size. It was accomplished piecemeal and, correspondingly, Muslim resistance was also piecemeal--but no less fervent for this reason.

The French destruction of the Kabyle uprising in 1871 (the year immediately after Picard's marriage to Sidi Ahmad) was the beginning of the end of Muslim resistance, although a silent hostility to the French smoldered underground and without direction until the Algerian Revolution of 1954 which finally led to independence in 1962. The French, in particular French settlers, had appropriated all the good agricultural land in the Tell so that the local Muslims had become merely outsiders looking in. No longer tribespeople, as their tribal cadres had been smashed, they were being turned even then into a rural peasant proletariat. The settlers, or pieds-noirs, (so nicknamed by the Algerians because of the short black boots most of them wore) became the core of the Présence Française in Algeria until the very end. To a large extent they were ignoble, small-minded people whose only objective was self-aggrandizement.

Local resistance to the French conquest was regional and sporadic. That of the Amir 'Abd al-Qadir was the best organized, of longest duration, and hence the best known. In an independent Algeria he has justifiably become the preeminent national hero, but whether he can legitimately be hailed as the first Algerian nationalist is open to question.

Muslim resistance was generally channeled through various religious orders (or tariqas) spread all over the country, all of them following a Sufi mystical approach to God and his Prophet Muhammad, one which was easily and quickly turned into a defence of Islam and its material and spiritual patrimony against the Christian invader.

The Qadiriya tariqa which, until his demise and surrender in 1847, was one of Amir 'Abd al-Qadir's main sources of support was one of these, while the Rahmaniya tariqa which was so thoroughly implicated in the Kabyle uprising of 1871 was another. But a third such tariqa, and a very powerful and influential one, the Tijaniya, had adopted a minority point of view and was in favor of French intervention. Why this was the case will be

4

discussed in Appendix A.

As Muslim religious orders go, the Tijaniya is quite recent, only two hundred years old. Its founder, Ahmad al-Tijani, or Sidi (my lord) Ahmad al-Tijani as he is referred to by his followers, was born in 1737 (1150 A.H.) in the south-central Algerian oasis of 'Ain Madi, located about sixty kilometers southwest of Laghouat. On his death in 1815 (1230 A.H.) it was to become one of the two seats of the order.

Although Abun-Nasr doubts Sidi Ahmad's claim to the title of sharif, or descendant of the Prophet Muhammad through the latter's daughter Fatima, he provides us with no evidence, genealogical or otherwise, to substantiate this observation. One should add that any doubtful aspects of the claim must be ones perceived through the lenses of modern scholarship, one which were and are in no way admitted by Sidi Ahmad's descendants or followers.[2] In the context of North African Islam, the title Sidi automatically means that its bearer is a sharif. In functional terms, if not necessarily in genealogical ones, any man is a sharif who is perceived to be such by the community at large; and this is so despite the fact that the traditional religious organization of the Maghrib (Muslim North Africa) is marked by a superabundance of shurfa (pl. of sharif).[3]

In any event Sidi Ahmad moved around considerably, in part no doubt to stay ahead of the Ottoman Turkish authorities with whom he never got on. He went to Fez in Morocco in 1757-8 then east to Mecca and made the hajj, the pilgrimage, in 1773-4, and afterward returned to Fez. From there he moved back into Algerian territory, first to Tlemcen in the northwestern part of the country and then all the way down to Sidi Bu Simghun, near 'Ain Sfra in the southwestern desert, in 1781-2 (1196 A.H.).

The history of the order dates from this time, for the Prophet appeared to Sidi Ahmad al-Tijani in a vision at Sidi Bu Simghun. The Prophet authorized him to begin his labors in guiding the spirits of men and designated to him the litany (wird) that his future order was to follow.

The Turkish authorities, however, were more suspicious than ever and they were able to expel him to Morocco in 1789. Whether or not his credentials as sharif are questionable, there is no question about his very genuine hatred of the Turks.

Sidi Ahmad remained in Fez until he died there in 1815 (1230 A.H.), although two years before his death he managed to revisit his birth-place at 'Ain Madi. It is recorded that even though the Fasis, the people of Fez, were hostile to him during his lifetime, his order took foot there and expanded, while a _zawiya_, a religious lodge-and-retreat-cum-shrine, was built over his mortal remains.

Before Sidi Ahmad's death, however, he appointed as his successor and head of the order a certain Sidi 'Ali bin 'Aisa al-Tamasini, from Tamasin, just south of Tuggurt and almost forty kilometers east of Laghouat and 'Ain Madi. On appointing this man, a local director, or the muqaddam, Sidi Ahmad al-Tijani stipulated that after his own death the leadership of the _tariqa_ should be held by both his own eldest male descendant and by that of Sidi 'Ali alternately: the point is one of crucial importance, because before 1820 it led to a major split between the two main lodges or _zawiyas_ of the Tijaniya at 'Ain Madi and at Tamasin or more precisely, at Tamalhat just south of it, where 'Ali bin 'Aisa took over the muqaddamship. Five decades later this split was to have major repercussions on the lives of Aurélie Picard and her husband Sidi Ahmad al-Tijani the Younger, the founder's grandson and fifth in line after him at 'Ain Madi.

After Sidi Ahmad's death--although presumably before a quarrel between his successors which resulted in his own descendants establishing themselves in 'Ain Madi while those of Sidi 'Ali went to Tamasin--Sidi 'Ali was able to persuade Sidi Ahmad's two sons, Muhammed al-Kabir and Muhammed al-Saghir (Muhammad the Elder and Muhammad the Younger respectively) to leave Fez and move to 'Ain Madi. Six months after the death of Sidi Ahmad, his sons returned to Fez in order to take their father's body to 'Ain Madi for re-burial, but the muqaddam of the Fez _zawiya_ was able to prevail on them to return the body to its shrine.[4]

So it happened that although Sidi Ahmad's body stayed in Fez, where the _zawiya_ became the object of pilgrimage by pious Tijaniya all over the Maghrib, the political and titular leadership of the order now moved over to Algeria, with the important result that the muqaddam of the Fez _zawiya_ no longer made any claims to act in the name of the order as a whole. But this is only one aspect of the wide-spread diffusion of the Tijaniya which now began; the other is the emergence of the order in areas far to the south, such as the Western Sudan (under Hajj 'Umar Tall), and in Senegal (under Hajj Malik Si and his descendants), and the further emergence, also in

West Africa, of dissident offshoot movements like the Hamalliya, which effectively prohibited any emergence of a single central authority after the death of the founder Sidi Ahmad. This was the case quite independently of the stance that the various branches of the order were to take on the issue of French colonialism--for those in West Africa were by and large wholeheartedly against it.

Although the _zawiya_ at 'Ain Madi stayed in the hands of Sidi Ahmad's descendants at his death, the top leadership of the Tijaniya order did not go to either of his sons, but to Sidi 'Ali bin 'Aisa al-Tamasini. Sidi 'Ali's family was a holy lineage based in Tamalhat near Tamasin, a large oasis in southeastern Algeria; and his father had met Sidi Ahmad in Cairo when both of them were on the return journey from the pilgrimage to Mecca. Though it was not without competition from other orders, it spread quite rapidly in Sidi 'Ali's time from Tamalhat to Gaymar further east in the same district, into the Tunisian Jarid, and into northern Tuareg country. Sidi 'Ali al-Tamasini followed the lead provided by Sidi Muhammad al-Saghir's (the Younger) friendly overtures to the French. In 1843-44 the Amir 'Abd al-Qadir's followers attacked Biskra, but its inhabitants were able to send a delegation to consult with Sidi 'Ali as to the wisdom of submitting peacefully to French authority. Sidi 'Ali replied in the affirmative, saying that French rule in Algeria was God's Will and that even though they were infidels they followed a just policy. Hence the Duc d'Aumale was able to pacify the Biskra area without bloodshed.

Oh Sidi 'Ali al-Tamasini's death the same year (1844), Sidi Muhammad al-Saghir, now leader of the order, visited the Tamasin _zawiya_ to assert his authority and to install muqaddams. The French, however, had begun to suspect him because letters from him to the son of the Sultan of Morocco were found in the latter's tent after his defeat by the French at Isli on August 14, 1844. These suspicions proved unfounded, and in May 1847 when Commandant Feray visited 'Ain Madi, Sidi Muhammad al-Saghir welcomed him into his house and even called on the army contingent at its camp and offered to say a prayer in the name of the French king.[5]

When Sidi Muhammad died in 1853 leadership of the Tijaniya returned to Tamasin with Sidi Muhammad al-'Aid (1814-76), Sidi 'Ali's eldest son. Sidi Muhammad al-'Aid collaborated with the French just as his father had done, helping the explorer

Duveyrier with letters to Tuareg chiefs and enabling him to travel over the Sahara as a member of the Tijaniya, and also helping to further French objectives in Tunisia.

But the reversion of the leadership to Tamasin was because Sidi Muhammad al-Saghir had left no sons by any of his legal wives. However, it was known that he had two black slave concubines, and one of these produced a son, named al-Bashir, shortly after his death. The other had left 'Ain Madi while pregnant three years earlier and also produced a son, who, if he could be found, was the rightful heir, as he was the elder of the two (an implicit admission of primogeniture, which normally has no primacy in Islam). Five years later the slave concubine and her son, named Ahmad, were located in Galma, near the Tunisian border; and Sidi Ahmad, the grandson and namesake of the founder, now became his father's successor as leader of the zawiya at 'Ain Madi.

When Sidi Ahmad succeeded to the Tijaniya leadership, the cautious and sometimes reluctant cooperation of his father Sidi Muhammad al-Saghir in his relations with the French was replaced by outright and total subservience.[6]

Only one event occurred to mar Sidi Ahmad's otherwise unblemished record in this respect. In 1888 he established contacts with a tribe of holy men (marabouts) known as the Awlad Sidi Shaikh who had been in continuous uprising against the French since 1864. He subsequently claimed to have done so only to safeguard the neutrality of those of his followers who resided among the insurgents, but the French refused to believe this story after the warriors of the Awlad Sidi Shaikh marched east to attack Laghouat, and Sidi Ahmad welcomed them at 'Ain Madi on their way.

It was thus that on February 1, 1869, General Sonis arrived at 'Ain Madi and defeated the Awlad Sidi Shaikh rebels as Sidi Ahmad and his brother looked on. After his victory General Sonis returned to Algiers, taking both Sidi al-Bashir and Sidi Ahmad with him as hostages in order to insure the good behavior of the other members of the order. It was Sidi Ahmad's captivity and enforced residence in Algiers that gave him the idea of a trip to France, where he conveyed the congratulations of fellow Muslims at home to the Muslim Algerian soldiers in the French army who had been through the battles of Wissembourg and Reichshoffen of the Franco-Prussian war. Immediately following his adroit maneuver he met Mlle. Aurelie Picard in Bordeaux.

We are fortunate in possessing in the work of Abun-Nasr an excellent study on the history, initial vicissitudes and external development of the Tijaniya Order in both North and West Africa. It is largely from his account that the groundlines of our own will be drawn.

> The story of the Tijaniya . . . offers an example (typical in some ways, though unique in many others) of the dilemma which faced the Sufi orders during the French period: desirous of preserving their hold on their followers they needed to curry favor with the French, who were the political masters of the society. But association with the "infidel" authorities was detrimental to their prestige . . . and gave their religious opponents, the Salafi fund- amentalists the opportunity to condemn them on both religious and political grounds. Their dilemma was much more difficult to resolve than that of the religious fundamentalists, whose posi- tion could be more clearly formulated and defended in the light of the Muslim faith, and who considered the French presence as a religious and national calamity which they would do everything possible to redeem and so accepted it grudgingly as long as they could not drive the French out. It was more difficult than that of the Westernized Muslims who had no tradition to preserve and often no faith to safeguard, and who either accepted the French presence as a necessity for belonging to Europe cul- turally or did not find the difference between a foreign and a Muslim ruler sufficiently important to justify their taking an interest in it. <u>The Sufi orders professed Islam, and in many ways considered themselves the guardians of the faith</u>: and the roles which they played in the African society did not permit them to take the easy and negative way out of emigration or of begrudging and thus hostile submission. Their story is, therefore, that of adjustment and reconciliation, which

9

would have enabled them to survive
politically had it not been that the
doctrine which they preached and the
functions which they performed were no
longer suited to modern times [i.e.,
that of the late nineteenth century].
[Emphasis mine.][7]

Chapter 2

EARLY LIFE IN FRANCE OF AURÉLIE PICARD
(1849-1870): HER MEETING AND
ENGAGEMENT TO SIDI AHMAD

Aurélie Picard came into the world on 12 June 1849, at a time when her parents had despaired of ever having children.

Her father had fought bravely in the campaigns of the conquest of Algeria and had been awarded the Legion of Honor. Sickness and fevers, however, sent him back to France. The damp, grey atmosphere of the Upper Marne made him nostalgic for the burning sun of Algeria and the harsh and exciting life of that country, so much so that with his health restored he was on the point of returning to Algeria to take advantage of the land commissions offered by a French government eager for colonists. With Aurélie's arrival this dream had to be abandoned. Four boys followed in quick succession and mid-nineteenth century Algeria was no place for pregnant women and babies fresh from Europe. With five children, life was hard for the Picards, especially when, toward the end of the Second Empire, Monsieur Picard retired from the army to become a poorly paid village policeman.

Little did the parents realize that their strong-willed daughter was destined to marry the head of a powerful Algerian religious order, become powerful herself, and live and die under the hot Algerian sun, having dedicated her life to the interests and service of France and Algérie Française.

Though Aurélie had no inkling of what the future held she became determined at a very young age that she would not be the drudge her mother was. At school she was neat, methodical, and assiduous in her studies, shining particularly in mathematics, natural science, and geography. But her domineering character made her unpopular. Furthermore, girls in her day were not meant to be studious, least of all those from poor families, and for that, too, she was

11

resented.

The dire financial straits of the Picard family obliged them to leave Moligny-le-Roi where Aurélie had been born and to move to Arc-en-Barrois where her father owned a meager plot of land and where they had a humble roof over their heads. By growing their own vegetables and raising whatever else they could find for themselves life became a little easier; study and school days, though, were over for Aurélie who had to work to help her family.

Aurélie became an apprentice in a dressmaking and millinery firm. Her days were spent ironing, opening and shutting doors for clients, and pinning dresses on discontented, grumbling rich women. At home in the evening she was expected to help her permanently tired mother with the washing and the housework and to run errands for her father. It was not a happy youth. The adolescent girl detested her family's poverty, and envy of the cold, hard, imperious women for whom she had to sew and wait upon burned in her heart; though she hated them and her lot she brooded upon becoming rich and authoritarian in her turn.

Escape from slavery she would, though the dreary treadmill was to continue until she was eighteen. Then one day Aurélie had her chance when an important and affluent grande dame, Mme Steenacker, who lived in an imposing chateau, came to the shop to choose some hats. Aurélie was told to wait on her, and Mme Steenacker, impressed by the girl's obvious superiority over her companions, insisted that she herself deliver the hats.

Aurélie arrived at the impressive residence and was ushered into a room to await Mme Steenacker. She was amazed at the opulence and luxury; so this was how the rich lived, she thought. She was far too nervous to sit down and Mme Steenacker laughed and chatted as Aurélie fitted the hats. Rings glittered on the lady's fingers and her bracelets jingled with every gesture.

Mme Steenacker questioned her about her job and Aurélie, with her innate astuteness, confessed that she was ill-suited to it and unhappy to have left her studies in order to help her parents. The lady's soft heart melted at Aurélie's plight and she proposed to employ her as her personal maid at a salary that seemed a fortune to Aurélie's frugal mind. Instinctively, Aurélie knew she was on the threshold of a new life and with alacrity accepted the job. Why consult her parents? After all, she was going up in the world.

They did not share Aurélie's convictions; where would being a lady's maid get her? Better to be trained in a career, however humble, than have no trade to fall back on, they argued. But the parents were up against Aurélie's implacable will, a will that was to take her far in life.

So she began her employment in the chateau, doing her best to please and be submissive, quelling her dominant will, dreaming that one day she, too, would be "someone." Aurélie set about observing carefully the ways and manners of those around her, of Mme Steenacker herself, listening to the way she spoke and gradually ridding herself of her strong regional accent. Mme Steenacker lent Aurélie books which she read avidly.

Despite Picard's comparative life of ease she never forgot her poor, hardworking parents to whom she faithfully turned over her wages. Father and daughter were very close, and while her father was still in the army and when she was quite young he had taught her to ride. Often while out he would talk to her of his days in Algeria and reminisce about the sights, sounds and smells of North Africa.

In 1870 war broke out between France and a newly unified Germany under the domination of Prussia, and the Steenackers were obliged to move with the government to Bordeaux. Aurélie was overjoyed to learn that she was moving with them as she could not bear the thought of going back to her old job and days of poverty once more. She accompanied Mme Steenacker in the family coach on her first long journey.

Aurélie was now twenty and still unaware that her life was to change dramatically; but she was not unaware of the strange Algerian Muslim guests who also had a suite in the requisitioned hotel. She eyed them discreetly, took in every detail of their exotic and costly robes; wherever they went they left a trail of dizzying perfume, while numerous black slaves in equally voluminous clothes followed behind these mysterious gentlemen who spoke in a harsh, guttural language. Images of her father's stories came to mind. She did not know that these flamboyant men were under house arrest and that one was the leading shaikh of the Tijaniya. The gentlemen were Sidi Ahmad al-Tijani and Sidi al-Bashir al-Tijani. The news of their arrival had preceded them and all of Bordeaux was agog. Their intended journey to France had been heralded in the French and Algerian press, and when the arrangements necessary for the pomp of such a journey were

13

completed the two brothers embarked on their voyage to Bordeaux via Paris.

They had never before traveled in a large ship, or across any water, for that matter, but when they encountered the train that was to take them to Paris they were truly stupefied, having never seen mile upon mile of straight steel vanishing into the distance nor endless telegraph cables that swooped up and down as the train sped past. The smoke, the noise and rattling and swaying of the carriages made them apprehensive and they were more than relieved when their journey came to an end.

News of their arrival was mentioned in the Algerian newspaper Le Mobacher which, on 19 September 1870 printed the following article.

> The marabouts of 'Ain Madi, Sidi Ahmad and Sidi al-Bashir, stayed for a while in Paris. Afterwards they traveled on to Bordeaux where General Damade gave them the warmest greetings. Once the people of Bordeaux learnt of the arrival of the Tijaniya brothers and the reason for their visit they massed in front of their residence to wish them a cordial welcome.[1]

They were the sensation of the city, being fêted everywhere they went. The Steenackers took Aurélie to a gala charity play to be performed in the brothers' honor. It was Aurélie's first visit to the theater.

Mme Steenacker had given her one of her simpler evening gowns and time off to alter it. Aurélie spent the whole afternoon in making herself beautiful; never had she been so happy. Slowly but surely she was getting nearer to her heart's desire--the glitter of the world of the rich.

Seated in a red velvet chair beside Mme Steenacker she surveyed the ornate sculptures and gold painted wood carvings and the immense, sparkling crystal chandeliers. Looking covertly at the other velvet-lined boxes Aurélie noted the elaborate coiffures, the wealth of the tiaras and the diadems as well as the costly rings and bracelets, to say nothing of the stunning uniforms of the officers who accompanied their wives and daughters.

Mlle Picard gazed down on the tiers of seats at the further gorgeous display of jewelry, silks, satins and the very latest in haute couture. The whole of Bordeaux was there. The rich, the famous, the elite and Mlle Aurélie Picard--a policeman's daughter. Although temperamentally she was cold and self-possessed, a wave of emotion engulfed her and a lump rose in her throat, and she who had never cried felt near to tears, though they would have been tears of triumph.

All at once, at a signal, the orchestra broke off its rendering of a currently fashionable air and burst into martial music. All eyes were drawn to the central box neighboring that of the Steenackers to where, with great pomp and ceremony, Sidi Ahmad al-Tijani and his brother made their way. With one accord the whole theater rose to welcome them, clapping long and vigorously. Sidi Ahmad smiled, and thanked the audience with bows and waves of his hand, and then, majestically, with a swirl of his robes, seated himself in the ornate armchair offered him; the lights slowly dimmed and all was silence.

The man whom the crowd applauded was not, as one might suppose, a handsome oriental prince and fair of face, for Sidi Ahmad had inherited the dark complexion and looks of his black mother. He was fat, with a flat nose, thick sensual lips, and a black frizzy beard which encircled his face. Only his eyes reflected kindness. Although only in his early twenties, he already had false teeth, the result of Arab negligence toward physical care and hygiene.

It might be imagined that without his glittering entourage and away from the official atmosphere that lent him the aura of a grand potentate, Sidi Ahmad would have lost all attraction. A French officer in the garrison at Laghouat described him, as weak and apathetic, with of a very mediocre intelligence, incapable of filling a role of considerable importance."

But that night Sidi Ahmad gloried in the prestige which effaced his gross features. The flowing drapes of his gold-embroidered, silk-lined burnous hid his corpulent body, his pudgy fingers were masked in sparkling rings, and chains of heavy silver set with jewels distracted the eye from a bulging neck. All this, along with the magnificence of the uniforms, the lace and velvet dresses and the light and music, combined to make a deep and lasting impression on Aurélie, an impression which no doubt weighed heavily in the choice of her destiny.

Next day Cinderella was back at work; the charm of the glittering evening was over, but far from forgotten. Among her duties was the care of Mme Steenacker's white doves, and as she took them through the hotel passages to the garden, she often caught sight of Sidi Ahmad and his escorts. Sidi Ahmad had become blasé because of his success and took not the slightest notice of the girl who watched him from afar.

However, one day, as he was just about to go out, magnificently arrayed, as usual, he came face to face with Aurélie bearing numerous white doves in her arms. Sidi Ahmad was brought up short by this graceful picture, which instantly and sadly reminded him of his own country where doves flew in hundreds free, around the delicate, slim minarets of the mosques. They are sacred birds in Islam, because one of them is held to have warned the Prophet Muhammad about approaching enemies. The young man stared at the dark and attractive girl who stood before him, her soft, glossy hair flowing in natural waves about her shoulders.

Aurélie noted the long look he gave her as he remained rooted to the spot, then she quietly and demurely moved on . . . perhaps a shiver of anticipation and premonition went through her as she continued on her way down the corridor. In her thoughts she no doubt relived that moment many times, but little did she guess to what extent she had captured the shaikh's attention. Since Aurélie had for some time observed his movements, had she not perhaps engineered this "meeting" making sure she would present an alluring picture, having carefully dressed her hair and awaited her moment?

Although at this time her sights were probably not set as high as Algeria or being in the service of France, she was no doubt thinking "Capture the present and that will shape the future."

It has been suggested that Mlle Picard may well have become Sidi Ahmad's mistress while he was in Bordeaux in order to keep him content and out of mischief; and that only later, after she became his wife, was she paid by the French intelligence service in Algeria from secret funds to spy for them and work in their interests. The question remains, for how else could a seamstress-cum-lady's maid with no private means have lived in such luxury and amassed such a fortune while married to a relatively impoverished head of a religious order. But that was in the future; Aurelie was now still just a slim, attractive girl of twenty.

In 1869-70 Aurélie had yet to learn abut the Tijaniya; 'Ain Madi and Tamasin were places of which she had never heard. Meanwhile Sidi Ahmad was in a quandary: he needed to get back to 'Ain Madi, but he

16

was already much taken with the amenities and pleasures of French living. In addition, he was infatuated with Aurélie, who now remained cold, distant and unresponsive to his smiles.

Sidi Ahmad had to go back to take control of affairs within the Tijaniya. Time was getting short and he was getting frantic as Aurélie played the game of avoiding him. In desperation he summoned up his courage and what little French he knew to ask for an interview with Mme Steenacker.

"Why do you suppose he wants to see me?" Mme Steenacker asked her companion breathlessly, her eyes shining. Aurélie acted indifferently though she was quite well aware of the real reason behind Sidi Ahmad's request. Mme Steenacker received Sidi Ahmad in the ornate drawing room of their suite.

Clumsily he explained his passion for Mlle Picard. Mme Steenacker was thunderstruck, though she maintained a calm exterior. Her ignorance of Muslim culture turned astonishment into horror when Sidi Ahmad announced that he would be willing to pay any price.

"But Aurélie is for marriage, not for sale!" declared Mme Steenacker angrily.

For that matter, marriage was not at all what Sidi Ahmad had envisioned to get the girl he wanted. From his life in France he saw that major cultural differences alone, to say nothing of religious ones, formed a serious barrier. He already had two wives in Algeria so how could he introduce a Christian woman as a third wife into the heart of the Tijaniya order? Concubinage, however, would present no difficulties. The head of the Tijaniya was nonplussed by Mme Steenacker's reaction and realized, vaguely, that by offering to buy Aurélie he had offended some mysterious Western custom. He excused himself humbly and repeated his protestations of love and passion.

"She is not my daughter," continued Mme Steenacker, "If your intentions toward her are serious you must speak to her father and ask him for her hand in marriage." And with that she abruptly ended the visit. The poor woman was worried, as she realized how much the shaikh coveted the girl. She told Aurélie of the conversation she had just held. Aurélie pretended surprise over Sidi Ahmad's admiration but was, in fact, uncertain about her own feelings for him. Mme Steenacker wrote forthwith to the Picard family explaining the situation and inviting them to Bordeaux.

In the meanwhile Sidi Ahmad was very preoccupied with obtaining authorization to return home, since the situation at 'Ain Madi was becoming more and more alarming. He tossed around in his mind for some way to prove his good faith toward the French and shake off the irksome yoke of house arrest, however lightly applied. In France it was easy for the establishment to keep an eye on him while giving him the key to the city. His authorization to visit France in the first place had been no spur-of-the-moment affair but a carefully worked out plan between Paris and Algiers to insure maximum benefit for the French.

Now that Sidi Ahmad wanted to leave and take command once more, the idea came to him that marriage to Aurélie might be a good thing after all. Given the sacrifice of Muslim law he was prepared to make--a particularly dangerous sacrifice for the head of a Muslim religious order and one which already stood out for subservience to the colonial establishment--the French might believe in his loyalty. Thus, despite his initial ardor, the marriage would be one of convenience.

M. Picard at first was not in favor of the union; having been in Algeria he had some idea of the religious and cultural differences between that country and France. Moreover, for all Sidi Ahmad's position, he lived in a desert village, possibly a refuge for dissident tribes and far removed from any European influence. Even so, he remembered and appreciated the charms of life in a Muslim country, and the idea of such a rich and powerful husband for his daughter was not altogether displeasing.

And what did Aurélie think? It was certainly not love at first sight, though love at the thought of power it certainly was. With her sheltered life as a maid and companion, Aurélie had never had an admirer. She must have fantasized about her ideal of a fiancé, and the man who had just asked for her hand must have been far from that ideal. What was being offered her in its place was a big step indeed. Was she ready to take it? The war was over and with innate astuteness she sensed she had become too big a responsibility for Mme Steenacker. To go back to Arc-en Barrios was out of the question; to marry a policeman and lead a poor, hardworking, frugal life, with, no doubt, a baby every year was impossible. She had no education and no dowry to offer a man who could keep her in the standard to which she had become accustomed.

If Aurélie accepted Sidi Ahmad's proposal she would be rich and everything that she had dreamed of

18

would be hers. Also she would see a new country
with blue and sunny skies. The thought of being
segregated in a harem never occurred to her--if she
even knew of the practice. She weighed the advantages and consented to be Sidi Ahmad's wife.

It was M. Picard now who dithered in giving
his consent as Sidi Ahmad became more pressing in
his demand. He sought advice from M. Steenacker who
was himself becoming restive over the drawn-out
decision. M. Steenacker declared impatiently,
"Don't you want your daughter, then, to make her
fortune?" And so it was decided.

That very day Sidi Ahmad was invited to the
Steenacker's suite. He sent ahead a magnificent
arrangement of flowers for Mme Steenacker and
dressed carefully in his most resplendent robes. He
was received in the private drawing room and sat on
a large couch with his interpreters at his side. M.
Picard entered the room accompanied by his daughter.
Despite a preliminary exchange of banalities the
atmosphere was strained and M. Picard inarticulate.
It was M. Steenacker who came to the point and
asked: "Aurélie, have you decided on your reply to
Sidi Ahmad's proposal?" Sidi Ahmad looked intently
at Aurélie who had not taken her eyes off him since
entering the room, as this was the first time she
had been quite so close to him.

He has nice eyes, she thought, but she
recoiled instinctively at his dark skin and frizzy
beard. Could she spend the rest of her life,
especially its intimacies, with that man? Now,
despite her initial decision, she hesitated. Her
father, irritated himself by her uncertainty,
demanded brusquely: "Well, Aurélie, what is your
answer?"

All eyes were upon her and Aurélie felt
suddenly trapped, caught in a vortex, and through
the whirling flashbacks of her childhood poverty
glittered the diamonds of her suitor. Sidi Ahmad
sensing her emotion and indecision, got up and
approached her gently, saying softly in broken
French, "Mademoiselle, I love you, all I have is
yours if you will be my wife and I swear you will be
happy." In his smile Aurélie saw warmth and tender-
ness, and his voice was so gentle that all her fears
vanished.

Aurélie smiled in her turn and in a resolute
voice replied: "I accept, Monsieur, to become your
wife." Sidi Ahmad bowed before her and took her
hand to kiss it. The contact froze Aurélie for a
moment and she shivered. But the hand that held

hers was warm and firm and velvety, and all of a sudden she found the touch exotically agreeable.

Amid the popping of champagne corks Aurélie was presented with a miniature jeweled casket inside of which rested a beautiful silver bracelet studded with precious stones, coral and turquoise. Aurélie Picard was astonished to note the speed with which she was already being spoilt. She suddenly relaxed and was surprised about her previous hesitation . . . Yes, indeed! She would be happy!

During the hubbub of felicitations M. Picard drew Sidi Ahmad aside with his interpreters; he insisted on certain conditions to the marriage for the protection of his daughter: such as marriage under French law and that he accompany her to Algiers where the ceremony was to take place. Sidi Ahmad agreed to everything, adding that the entire cost of the journey would be paid for by him, for would not Aurélie's family now be part of his own?

Sidi Ahmad was allowed to pay court to his betrothed. The courtship was difficult because Sidi Ahmad's French was bad and Aurélie herself had to learn Arabic through an interpreter who was not always helpful. But words were not needed to convey Sidi Ahmad's tender solicitude and love. He showered her with costly gifts which at first she was reluctant to accept.

Sidi Ahmad hid nothing from her of his past life, nor the fact that he had two legitimate wives still in 'Ain Madi. To a less audacious girl this knowledge might have caused some worrying moments, but having basked in luxury she planned to hang on to it, and so she bided her time until such "details" would be arranged to her own satisfaction.

With the Affaire Picard nicely under way the Tijaniya brothers at last obtained their long-awaited authorization to leave France. It came straight from the top, from General MacMahon, the future president of France. So the brothers and their retinue embarked along with Aurélie and her father, to sail for Algiers and marriage. Aurélie was far too happy to have any pangs of sadness as she watched the coast of France fade away. In any case she would serve it diligently as a voluntary exile for the following sixty years.

What thoughts crossed her mind? Did she wonder whether she would see her mother or family or village again? Probably if she thought such thoughts she banished them and with the unlimited confidence of her twenty years faced a new and dazzling future.

Chapter 3

AURÉLIE PICARD AND SIDI AHMAD TIJANI (1870-1883)

It is uncertain whether Aurélie was Sidi Ahmad's mistress while still in France, but she certainly seems to have become so shortly after her arrival in Algiers. They were lodged for a few days in a hotel, and then she and her father were moved into a sumptuous urban Arab mansion. Aurélie was quite overcome with the exquisite delicacy of the mosaic walls, the great painted and carved beams and spacious rooms that opened out on to white marble terraces adorned by cool fountains tiered like a wedding cake. Beautiful landscaped gardens fell away to the brilliant blue Mediterranean. It was a wonderland of color, and there was nothing in the gray austerity of France to compare with it.

However, everything in the garden was not lovely. Back once more on home territory, Sidi Ahmad was no longer the fêted foreign prince, but a man expected to do as he was told. First he had to get authorization to live in the house with Aurélie,[1] because the colonial establishment in Algeria, and hence French rule there, was still military, despite an increasingly powerful civilian and settler lobby. After the 1870 Franco-Prussian War and the 1871 Kabyle uprising, the army began to fade into the background, at least in the Tell. Furthermore, what Sidi Ahmad did not tell Aurélie when he went to live in the house, probably because he was unaware of it, was that at the time (1870) cross-religious marriages between French Christians and Algerian Muslims were statutorily not allowed.

Meanwhile strengthened by the success of his mission in France and the good graces in which he stood with the French authorities, he went to see the governor-general, Admiral Louis Gueydon, to get special permission to marry Aurélie. Gueydon turned him down flat, saying "An Arab marry a Frenchwoman! Never! I am absolutely opposed to it."[2]

This must have come as a real slap in the face to Sidi Ahmad--a man of consequence in his own land,

21

even though he was also a collaborationist. After all the encouragement they had received in France, Aurélie was shocked to encounter such strong opposition in Algeria, not only from the French, but also from Sidi Ahmad's own people. Not least of this opposition came from his own interpreter who did a complete about-face, chiefly because he had designs on Sidi Ahmad marrying his own daughter. Being fully aware of the conditions of marriage that had been drawn up and to which Sidi Ahmad had agreed, particularly to the clause of only one wife, the interpreter dearly wanted to oust Aurélie or prevent an actual marriage.

Authorization was withheld by the French for at least two reasons: (1) because no one knew what the fate of this Frenchwoman would be once she was "exiled" in the Sahara without a single compatriot or recourse to help should she need it and (2) the revolt fomented by Sidi Muhammad al-Muqrani and Shaikh al-Haddad in Kabylia had not yet been squashed. To the contrary, it seemed as though rebellious tribal bands would soon be marching threateningly toward Algiers, so it is probable that Gueydon was not kindly disposed toward Sidi Ahmad. Since things were not going at all well, Sidi Ahmad Tijani turned to the qadi (judge) to marry them according to Qur'anic Law. But the qadi refused and in the following terms:

> I am forbidden to perform civil acts of marriage between Europeans and Algerian Muslims; and what you are proposing is nothing more than an act of marriage to a European. As marriage involves two people, the husband as well as the wife, this means that if I were to give you a marriage certificate it would have to be entered in the register. And this means I would be giving you a certificate I am not allowed to issue, a marriage act between a Muslim and a European woman.[3]

Sidi Ahmad was furious. He did not believe the qadi's reason for refusing to marry them and took him to court, where his case was again turned down. The case now went before the Court of Appeal in Algiers which, on 24 October 1871, confirmed the qadi's statement that he only had the right to marry Muslims to each other. Nonetheless the fact that the matter went to two successive French courts is a clear indication of how Muslim law and legal

22

procedure might be superseded under the colonial establishment.

Aurélie's father now began to regret having given his consent, and suggested it would be better for Aurélie to return to France. Possibly he began to wonder if she would ever become an "honest" woman. Aurélie refused to return to France. It had seemed so easy in her country--in fact it had been agreed that Aurélie would be the forfeit for Sidi Ahmad's liberty (and that of his brother). Now the French authorities in Algiers would have none of this and remained adamant and impervious to whatever Bordeaux may have arranged--an indication again of the administrative autonomy of Colonial Algeria.

As a last resort Sidi Ahmad remembered the calling card he had been given by Cardinal Charles-Martial Allemand-Lavigerie when the latter was visiting Bordeaux. Lavigerie was the founder of the Society of the White Fathers and he was most sympathetic to the couple's cause, as he judged the union between Sidi Ahmad and Aurélie Picard invaluable for the work of proselytization among the Muslims of Algeria (an important objective of his Society, particularly among the Berber-speaking Kabyles, regarded as riper targets for eventual Christianization than the Arabs). Therefore, he offered to marry the couple in the Roman Catholic Church. As there was nothing the qadi could now do about it, Sidi Ahmad and Aurelie married first in a Christian ceremony and then according to the <u>Shari'a</u> by the Mufti of the Hanafi rite in Algiers, Sidi Bu Qandura.[4] This action must have infuriated the authorities but there was nothing they could do as the cardinal was above official sanction. It meant, however, that Aurélie would not have the protection of French civil marriage laws.

There followed exhausting days of interminable feasting, dancing, and music. To Aurélie's staid Second Empire, or Victorian, mind the lascivious, suggestive and erotic dancing must have been highly shocking, though she maintained her usual outward calm and reserve. She was the only woman visible among all the male guests, the other ladies of the harem being veiled and segregated behind small latticed windows from where they, too, watched the festivities . . . and Aurélie.

Picard perceived from the very beginning that her main physical attraction and her later ascendancy over Sidi Ahmad lay in the fact that her European clothes made her different from any Algerian Muslim woman. She wore the loosely flowing extravagant dress and baggy trousers only for fun, otherwise remaining in the stiffly formal fashions of the Second Empire. Her only indulgence was jewelry which she wore lavishly no matter how simple the dress or occasion.

Instinctively she knew that she should begin from the start to live as a Frenchwoman. Not for her the veil, seclusion and outward docility; and anyway docility was not in Aurélie's nature. As a foreigner in a small Saharan village the safety of her life would depend on the strength of her will.

The journey from Algiers to 'Ain Madi took twenty days, and what a journey it must have been! The usual method of travel for Muslim women in the Sahara was in a covered basur or "cage" on top of a camel. Aurélie was afraid of camels and refused to travel this way. She was, however, a good horse-woman and, dressed in the sidesaddle habit of the day, she mounted a white mare that she had forced her husband to select and have saddled for her and rode with him at the head of their immense cavalcade toward her future home in 'Ain Madi. Sidi Ahmad was scandalized about the mare, but there was evidently nothing he could do; argument was to no avail.

The cortege was no doubt most impressive with Sidi Ahmad at its head dressed more gloriously than any other gentleman present. A line of spirited horses pranced along decked out in richly embroider-ed harness, with gold and silver embroidered velvet blankets beneath high-backed saddles while silver stirrups glinted in the sunlight. The loaded baggage camels were no less colorful, and their embroidered panniers with bright woollen tassels swayed with each stride. They were led by black slaves, and atop many of them were the women of the household swaying sickeningly inside their basurs. In the center of all this, Aurélie rode unveiled, straight and firm on her glossy white mare, survey-ing with interest all around her as though this arduous journey were no more than a canter in the Bois de Boulogne.

Except for the opulent mode of travel, Aurélie felt as though she might still be in France. She encountered French-style farm houses and land under cultivation by the ever-increasing influx of settlers. The flourishing vineyards, orange groves and olive plantations were all enchanting and nostalgic to Aurélie's French eyes. As they climbed higher the evenings and early mornings held a nip of autumn--for it was already September--and the rustling poplars that lined the frequent streams

24

were turning yellow.

They were welcomed in every little town and village they passed through, everyone begging to accommodate the young French bride, the wife of the sharif; there was no lack of shelter, be it a simple mud house or the fine mansion of a country qaid, or squire. When the houses faded away as they penetrated further and further south into the desert, tents were then put up. This was no simple, ordinary affair, for now the baggage camels were always a lap ahead; and when Aurélie, Sidi Ahmad and his retinue (and of course the hidden ladies) rode in, a splendid encampment awaited them. The air was rich with the aroma of roasting sheep, and in front of the notables' tents gleamed the heavily embossed silverware of tea services. The tents themselves were furnished with low tables, brass trays on legs, and valuable carpets which hid the hard-baked sand.

All along the way, Sidi Ahmad's baraka (God-given blessing) was clamored for, from veiled women as well as men. This was an astonishing experience for Aurélie, who was amazed by the exultant cries as her husband gave his benedictions and also by the crowds pressing to touch his clothes, his feet, his hands; she now began to realize just how important and powerful a man her spouse really was.

So they leisurely traversed the silent, stony desert across which the wind blew constantly. Despite the length of the journey, Aurélie never appeared to tire, and her clothes always looked immaculate in spite of the dust and heat. Sumptuous evening banquets seemed to be the rule of the voyage, and the nights throbbed to drums and music and dancing. Aurélie, in fact, found the music discordant and displeasing but she had to smile and bear it as it was all a tribute to her husband's importance; and that was what mattered. The desert nights and mornings were now bitterly cold and always there was further and still further to travel. "We're almost there," encouraged Sidi Ahmad, his elation very evident.

Finally repeated cries of "'Ain Madi! Al-hamdu lillah!" (Praise be to God!) bellowed forth from the cortege, and there it was an ochre blob in the far, flat distance. Excitement surged through Aurélie as the inhabitants poured out of the village, led by Sidi al-Bashir (Sidi Ahmad's younger brother who had returned home on arrival in Algiers). In a wild gallop they greeted their lord by firing off their flintlocks, and as they approached on their equally excited horses ululated

25

and yelled from the ramparts.

Aurélie was deeply shocked at her first sight of the all-important 'Ain Madi. To her European eyes it was nothing but a barbaric mud fortress. Was <u>this</u> where she was expected to live? Indeed she was on her own: far from help or rescue in this alien desert, her stout heart must have quailed somewhat.

'Ain Madi, Aurélie Tijani's new home, is thus described by Léon Roches as it appeared some thirty years before she first saw it; at the time it was besieged by 'Abd al-Qadir. In those thirty years it had probably hardly changed.

> The town was enclosed within a circular wall 20-30 feet high and more than 12 feet thick with a parapet on top about 8 feet wide. This parapet formed a path along which the lookout could walk. The wall was pierced by narrow slits for guns (or people to peek from) and around its periphery were twelve further turrets jutting out about six feet from which a rain of fire could pour down on the assailants at the foot of the wall. To the left and right were two more fortresses at least twenty meters high, divided into two floors. The town had two entrances, one to the west and one in the middle; the double doors being reinforced with iron on the top of which was a crenelated rampart. A narrow walled path led to an interior fortress which was again protected by a solid, impregnable door. These fortifications were built about thirty years ago [1840, approximately] by a Tunisian. The present-day walls are less strong--but the protection of France is sufficient.[5]

To Aurélie, her residence appeared more like a prison than a palace, and seldom did the women ever leave it. A woman, Arabs maintain, should only see the sky and the inside walls of her house. After the sumptuous life her husband had led in modern comfort both in Bordeaux and in Algiers it was, indeed, a rude awakening. Possibly it was the height of comfort to the locals, but to a bride with a French upbringing the dwellings appeared little more than hovels. Hairy spiders draped their cobwebs from every pillar; servants abounded and

still the place was filthy. Dust, never disturbed
by a broom or a cloth, lay thick over costly
carpets, silver-engraved weapons, and furniture; and
amongst all this neglected wealth dirty cooking
utensils lay scattered about.

It did not take the resilient Aurélie long to
figure out what might be in it for her. She quickly
calculated that it was very probable that such
wealth, ignored and neglected, had never been inven-
toried or checked since the death of Shaikh Muhammad
al-Saghir, the father of the two present shurfa.
And now a further shock awaited Aurélie: two wives
of Sidi Ahmad were still in residence at 'Ain Madi.
She was instantly jealous of them, and they must
have been even more so of her and, no doubt, planned
to poison her, a Christian and an infidel. At her
instigation, and invoking the contract drawn up by
her father and husband, she insisted that the women
were to be divorced and banished. In 1872, Sidi
Ahmad divorced his first wife, Raqiya bint Si
Muhammad, the daughter of his paternal uncle. Then,
considerably later, he divorced his second wife,
Salti bint 'Umar, though she defied Aurélie and
continued to live on at 'Ain Madi, remaining a thorn
in Aurélie's side. Sidi Ahmad deceived Aurélie in
pretending that he only had two wives, and she hit
the roof when she learnt of an unknown third wife,
Zuhra, who gave birth to a son in the spring of
1879. For over a year, such scenes of jealous fury
followed that Sidi Ahmad promised to divorce her
too, but in this Aurélie did not quite have her way.
At the insistence of some of his advisors he
refrained from divorcing Zuhra, although this wife
had to leave. Sidi Ahmad sent Zuhra to Tlemcen on
the pretext of having her watch over the interests
of her father's zawiya as he had died in June 1878.
To be certain that there was no more cheating on
home ground, Aurélie herself accompanied Zuhra to
Tlemcen, though the boy, 'Ali, remained with his
father, as prescribed by Muslim law, and Aurélie
brought him up as her own son.[6] Meanwhile, Mme
Tijani, as she now was to be generally become known,
determined to liberate the women of the harem from
what she considered a living death. She never
stopped to wonder if they wanted to be liberated
and, if liberated, what they would do. The husbands
most certainly did not want liberated wives! She
had already fanned up anger and jealousy on the part
of the female relatives of the banished wives; and
probably that of her mother-in-law, a black woman
from Galma. Aurélie was possibly unaware that

27

although an Arab woman has no external authority, she holds a very considerable power as a mother over her son even after he has become a man: for as mother-in-law she is the head of the women's quarters and a person whose dominance is uncontested. Indeed, literature is replete with examples supporting the views that to her son's wife, in particular, she can be a holy terror!

It is a strain for any woman anywhere to meet her in-laws for the first time; and the way in which they descended en masse on Aurélie must have been a cultural ordeal to which only her strong self-discipline was able to stand up. Through al-Bashir's earlier arrival in 'Ain Madi, the news of Sidi Ahmad's fourth marriage, this time to a Frenchwoman, spread like wildfire. Because of the scandal, the horror, the excitement, everyone wanted to go to 'Ain Madi; for none had ever seen a Frenchwoman, or any Christian woman (_rumiya_ or _nasraniya_), for that matter.

There were fourteen sisters-in-law to meet, all of whom announced their intention of arriving together. Then there were the daughters, now elderly women and power-wielders in their own way, of the late Sidi Muhammad al-Saghir. All were married to muqaddamin (pl. of muqaddam) of the Tijaniya, from its various daughter _zawiyas_ in the north-central and the eastern Algerian Sahara, which in those days were many weeks of travel away, so the visit would be a long one. In addition, there were the daughters of all these venerable ladies. Agog with curiosity, this well-escorted caravan of ladies set out across the desert, each with her own retinue of female slaves and coffers full of precious stones, gold and jewelry . . . one might think that this would have been quite a haul for bandits or enemy tribesmen, but as the women were the daughters of a descendant of the Prophet and were themselves the wives of influential members of the order, their lives and property were sacrosanct.

Aurélie, resolved she would show this inquisitive, hostile crowd of females how a Western woman dressed and acted, remained outwardly calm and unperturbed in what were to them her strange and stiff foreign clothes. They were insolent, snickering and laughing at her openly. However, when the master entered the room, they became sweet and docile. Aurélie felt far removed from them. Convinced of her moral superiority, she was completely at ease in the presence of this much feared shaikh.

The women attempted to pronounce her unfamiliar, foreign name, but gave up and decided to call her Lalla Yamina. "Who was Lalla Yamina?" queried Aurélie, and Sidi Ahmad replied: "Lalla Yamina was the daughter of a king of Tunisia that Sidna 'Abdallah, the chief general of the Prophet, Muhammad, married and took back with him to Mecca." This pleased Aurélie, so with her high self-opinion she accepted the name she was given. But, adamantly Western, she made no effort to learn about the life that her namesake had lived so that she could model her own upon it. She continued to live as no Arab Muslim woman had ever lived, according to a French lifestyle with plenty of positive, fruitful activity. Not only did she preserve her French outlook, but little by little she brought some of the more traditional and recalcitrant members of the order round to her way of thinking. What to her seemed the nonchalant, drifting way of life of her sisters-in-law only further confirmed her aspirations. The empty pleasures with which these confined women of the desert lulled themselves had no attraction for her and could never have filled her days. Long siestas on overstuffed cushions in dark rooms that buzzed with flies, the murmur of running water that drop by drop wore away at the fountain irritated her, as did the prattle of the women who endlessly threaded jasmine flowers and envied each other's jewelry. For entertainment the ladies peered from behind the grills of tiny windows at the powder plays, the acrobats and snake charmers and the sensuous dancing of the girls from the Awlad Na'il. Girls from this tribe near Laghouat specialize in dancing and prostitution before settling down to marriage. In the normal European stereotype she thought that an indolent kind of life might be bearable for lazy Arab minds, but it was certainly not so for her and her vigorous mentality.

Once the female guests from the east had left, Aurélie lost no time in putting into effect some of the projects close to her heart. She introduced bed linen into the household, French-style food which she cooked herself and chairs to sit on rather than cushioned divans which she considered bad for the posture. Her desire was to surround herself and Sidi Ahmad with Western comforts and an atmosphere that would bring back the days of Bordeaux, days of exile maybe, but also days of love.

However, such a transformation would have been impossible at 'Ain Madi. Too much venerable dust would have been disturbed and it aroused the mistrust of the elderly notables for whom Aurélie was nothing more than a capricious love affair of the young shaikh and over which they preferred to draw a veil.

Aurélie felt stifled by this atmosphere of disapproval and hostility. The Christian concubine (as she was considered) of the head of the Tijaniya wanted to leave the very closed society and al-Bashir and his cohorts in the "holy city" of 'Ain Madi. She was ready to move to Laghouat where Sidi Ahmad owned a palace and where she could spend the major part of her time. It was a judicious choice for another reason, as the small Arab village of Laghouat clung to the flanks of two hills which were crowned by a pair of fortresses from which fluttered the Tricolor and in which there was a French garrison. In Laghouat she was to spend many long weeks relieved of the oppression that smothered her. She was away from the antagonism of 'Ain Madi and spent many carefree, intimate days with Sidi Ahmad, free from malevolent looks and eavesdroppers. Aurélie used her ascendancy over Sidi Ahmad so skillfully that she obtained complete charge over everything pertaining to the house. Her slaves and retinue were greatly in awe of her and when she scolded them, though they understood not a word, they were afraid. Not the smallest grain of dust escaped her eyes, for Aurélie was a strict disciplinarian. It is interesting that Bassenne in Princesse des Sables, published before Aurélie Picard's death and based to some extent on interviews with her, comments uncritically and in purple prose on the goodness and sweetness of Aurélie's nature, whereas Crosnier in Aurélie Picard gives an opposite view, that she was hard, acquisitive and had a viperish tongue. Certainly the archival materials show that Crosnier's view was closer to the mark. And Aurélie Picard, convinced as ever of her superiority over her entourage, determined to expand her field of activities, to gain more independence for herself and to exert what she felt was her right over the native population by a "civiliz-ing" (French) influence among the nomads of the l-Arba' whose spiritual allegiance was to the shaikh.

However, Picard was not given to hasty actions; with due reflection she realized that the way to obtain influence would be in doing good turns to the Tijaniya and persuading her husband, and after him, the muqaddmin of the order that they would gain through seeking her advice. First of all she set herself to working on her Arabic and learn-ing as much as she could about the doctrine and

30

history of the order to whose shaikh she was married.

The more Aurélie learnt about the religious life of the _zawiya_, the more interested she became. Pilgrims from the Congo to Tunisia came to pay their respects at the tomb of Sidi Muhammad al-Saghir. They were blistered by the sun, sick and covered in sores. They came to try to obtain bits of his _baraka_ and that of Sidi Ahmad, and they might even have believed that Aurélie had acquired some of this same _baraka_ and could thus help heal them. Through common sense and Western hygiene she bandaged their wounds, bathed sore eyes, and applied simple country treatments which she had learnt as a girl in France. She ordered medicines from Algiers. The work was hard in the beginning as her remedies were viewed with hostility and suspicion, especially among the women who were convinced that the pills and potions were _haram_, forbidden. In secret they washed off her ointments, and the bandages adorned and fluttered around the _marabout_'s tomb; but gradually the braver and more experimentally-minded among the pilgrims endured her remedies, no doubt in order to prove the Christian woman wrong only to discover that her medicines were often effective.

Any study of the holy books was closed to Mme Tijani since they were in Arabic and in an ornate calligraphic script. In the library of the _zawiya_ were shelves of Arabic manuscripts covered thick with the dust of years. Aurélie left them undisturbed as it sufficed her to question people around her at 'Ain Madi when she stayed there; she had now become quite proficient in spoken Arabic and was able to become closely acquainted with the religious life of the village in order to become a good counsellor to Sidi Ahmad. The Shaikh, proud of his auspicious house, continued to instruct Aurelie in the life, history, traditions and precepts of his order. And, just as she had been as a schoolgirl, Aurélie proved an adept pupil.

Slowly, Aurélie gained a reputation as a healer as well as the complete confidence of her husband, through whom she controlled the purse strings. He came to have complete faith in his spouse's advice and her policies in the administration of the _zawiya_, principally through the acquisition of _ziyara_ donations given annually to Sidi Ahmad by his constituents. Acquisition is certainly the operative word, for in 1883-84 a group of l-Arba' with their camels came to offer their _ziyara_ to Sidi Ahmad. While they were performing

31

their devotions in the _zawiya_, Mme Aurélie had the camels branded and sent them off to join her husband's herds. After some hesitation, not wanting to speak to the saint himself, the pilgrims reported what had happened to the Bureau Arabe (local French office for the administration of native affairs) in Laghouat. The officer who received them declared that he had noted their complaint against the saint, that the latter would be asked to return the camels and that pressure would be brought to bear if he refused. When they heard this, the l-Arba' backed down and stated formally that they would refuse to bring a legal action against a Tijani and that they preferred to let him have the camels. They retired and were not seen again![7]

On the subject of Sidi Ahmad's adviser, Qaid Rihan, it is necessary to backtrack three decades.[8] Once Turkish rule in Algeria was finished, though after 'Abd al-Qadir's election to the sultanate, Sidi Muhammad al-Saghir quickly let it be known to the French army command in Algeria, that he wanted to create a Tijani polity in the south-central part of the country. However, he delayed making explicit overtures to the French until after 'Abd al-Qadir's siege of 'Ain Madi. In July 1839 he wrote a letter to Marshal Valee stating explicitly that in return for arms and help, he would undertake to collect legal alms and taxes imposed by the Qur'an from the local population and would assist the French in imposing their domination over the "ignorant Bedouins," pointedly referring to 'Abd al-Qadir as their chief and calling him a man who knew nothing of relations between statesmen. Even though they did not answer his letter, the French nonetheless decided to make use of Sidi Muhammad's offer of alliance.[9]

When in November 1840 Sidi Muhammad al-Saghir al-Tijani returned to the town of 'Ain Madi, he called upon all the people of the neighborhood to help rebuild the village. Many strangers arrived who were given the houses and gardens of the people who had abandoned the Tijani cause. A month later the people returned to find their properties taken over and themselves at the mercy of Sidi Muhammad. Qaid Rihan, an old friend of Sidi Muhammad and also a stranger to 'Ain Madi, had become the tutor to the young Sidi Ahmad and Sidi al-Bashir. In his elevated position of tutor and qaid he proceeded to usurp a great deal of land belonging to 'Ain Madi people, and then lined his pockets further by selling it off, to the fury of the helpless villagers who were unable to return to it. He also appropriated two nights' worth of irrigation water which he used on his gardens. What remained of his allotments he sold off for forth to fifty duros a month, a considerable sum of money at that time.

Theft of land and water are two unforgivable sins and Rihan's doings soon came to the ears of the commandant of the region. He called Rihan in and ordered him to return all the money illegally obtained. There were long arguments and refusals, Rihan still clung to what was not legally his, and though he still continued to line his pockets, he did so less blatantly. This was more or less the situation until Aurélie Picard Tijani came on the scene, suspected what was going on, and began to put matters right with a very firm hand.

With her practical turn of mind and organizational abilities she felt particularly capable of advising Sidi Ahmad on the order's finances which in the zawiya were closely interwoven with religious affairs. Sidi Ahmad, his family, and the members of the 'Ain Madi order lived on the tithes and ziyara donations which also were meant to sustain the poor. From these revenues, too, Sidi Ahmad kept up the order's prestige abroad. By running the household and becoming aware of its day-to-day expenditures, Aurélie soon become aware of the chaotic state of the order's finances, ground away by a cloud of parasites. It seemed to her that with an effective accounting system to repress abuses, the order's resources could be used more equitably for the benefit of the poor and the proteges of the Tijaniya Zawiya.

Sidi Ahmad's authority as shaikh was, of course, the key to setting matters straight, but care had to be taken to avoid upsetting the traditionalists. No clumsy mistakes could be made by the shaikh's wife. Before beginning her reforms, Aurélie wanted to learn, in depth, how the order functioned, from where its wealth came, who disposed of it and how, and what the founder had intended as the order's mission.

Chapter 4

BUILDING OF QURDAN: TUNISIAN AIMS AND
DEATH OF SIDI AHMAD (1883-1897)

The nomads had gotten over their shock and become used to seeing Aurélie riding freely over the countryside. For her it was a relaxation from her arduous duties; she loved to go out hunting on horseback with her husband, often, indeed, with falcons as they galloped after hares, gazelles and ostrich (the last-mentioned, unfortunately, now long gone from the Northern Sahara). In this way she came to know the environment very well.

There was a spring in the region of 'Ain Madi where the air was relatively cool and the sandy ground damp. Husband and wife often refreshed themselves at this spring and whiled away the stifling hours beneath an immense fig tree. The site was known locally as Qurdan.

Aurélie allowed herself to dream and scheme. This would be the ideal place to create a garden in the desert, a European creation of fruit plantations, vegetables in a wide scale, grains and . . . flowers! The blooms that would remind her of France, the country that was never far from mind, and from that very country she would order the seeds. Her thoughts raced ahead, strong, patronizing, and colonial as usual.

No sooner was the idea conceived than it became an extravagant project. She would build a French-style house where she would be absolute mistress, free to order and do as she liked. A clear-sighted look at their personal financial resources revealed that what they had was only a drop in the bucket compared to the gigantic sums required to build a place worthy of the head of the Tijaniya. Her thoughts turned toward funds from the zawiya, but, though the gifts from the faithful were numerous, there was barely enough money to support the extravagant household of 'Ain Madi, and Sidi Ahmad dared not dip into it for a personal enterprise.

Cost what it may, Aurélie was set on achieving her heart's desire. To this end, and with her husband's approval, she set off as his ambassador to Algiers to plead for the desired property to the governor general. She put forward her grandiose ideas eloquently, perceptively explaining the benefits which employment would bring to an almost destitute people, people dependent for their well being on the whims of the seasons. Further she added cunningly, that in return for employment on such a scale the people would feel beholden to France, would consider her their benefactress, and once the project was completed, would enjoy an improved standard of living. This could not be denied. For her part, and at the request of the government, she and Sidi Ahmad were to be responsible for pro-French propaganda going out to the Tunisian zawiyas with a view to a smooth occupation there, and indeed to the zawiyas in the Western Sudan as well. (French attempts at utilizing the Tijaniya toward colonial ends backfired badly, however, because the order in West Africa was very hostile, and its communications with the Algerian mother zawiyas were minimal.[1]) Aurélie returned to Laghouat proud and happy to have secured French financial backing for the building of the house at Qurdan. At a later date, she made a further journey to Algiers to get together the necessary materials and select the right wood for the carpenters to start the construction of Qurdan. As transport for the materials, a convoy of fifty baggage camels accompanied her while Aurélie rode on horseback in her accustomed style. With her efficiency only one visit to the capital was necessary; Mme Tijani knew her orders would be carried out to the letter, and the rest of the project could be supervised from Qurdan, far as it was.

The discerning reader might now be wondering if Aurélie Picard Tijani might not have been in the pay of French Intelligence. One is strongly inclined to think so, and suspect that she was recruited by them virtually as soon as she was married to Sidi Ahmad.

We base this supposition on two facts which are obvious and on our own inference, which is less so. The facts are: (1) all of Picard's actions were fully in line with and consistent with French colonial policy in the Algerian Sahara, and were hence almost certainly dictated by that policy, and (2) a great deal of money obviously went into financing the whole operation at Qurdan, and this money could only have come from funds allocated by the French Intelligence-gathering operations, as Picard had no private means. The inference is drawn from the observation that much of the archival material concerning her, whether in Aix-en-Provence, Paris or Bordeaux is still classified information and is not yet available to scholars.

In 1883 Aurélie's great project began. It was an ambition that would take ten years to achieve and in which acres of desert would be transformed into lucrative, productive, and fertile land. It was through Aurélie's inexhaustible drive to turn nomads into sedentary agriculturalists that the order began to gain new economic vitality. Mme Aurélie, with an eye to material gain, firmly controlled the purse strings and handled all the Tijaniya accounting.

Despite the fact that Aurélie employed the best available French architects, engineers and agriculturalists, she supervised everything and dominated everyone. Fresh veins of water were uncovered and hectares of land were put under irrigation. Where the sound of flowing water had scarcely ever been heard, it now become commonplace. The plantations grew; the calls of birds filled the air; maize and cereals flourished, were harvested, planted and flourished again. Two crops a year in that fine climate, with unlimited water, were easily produced. In this newly created oasis permanent dwellings rose and became the village of Qurdan; as the land was claimed the nomad tents moved further out into the desert.

It was here Aurélie wanted to live, in the middle of her creation, in order to keep it under close surveillance. Thus it was with no regrets that she left the discomforts of the old house in which she had lived for so many years. Qurdan was to become her dream house: a Western house built under the direction of a master mason brought all the way from Algiers. This house was her glory and joy, with its ample bay windows, balustrade terraces, cupolas, crenelated milky-white walls, and secluded courtyards covered in tiled mosaics. Except for the walls which were made from local stone and the locally made carpets (which no doubt had accrued to the shaikhs over the course of various generations), all was imported from the Tell, and some antiques were supposedly imported from the Far East.

Thousands of mosaics, carved cedar wood, iron grilles and art treasures were laboriously brought to Qurdan by camel trains, weeks of travel over

terrible tracks. We provide the following quotation
from Bassenne:

> One can understand that the building
> and fitting out of this villa was a feat
> of strength from the all-powerful
> Frenchwoman.
> Seventy-six servants, black and
> white, were required to run the house,
> all under the energetic supervision of
> the mistress of the house herself, for
> the greater comfort of her guests. And
> her French guests were particularly
> numerous. Any Frenchman traveling in
> the region who expressed a desire to see
> the riches and wonders of Qurdan was
> overwhelmed by lavish entertainment.
> Governors of Algeria, French
> generals and other officers, explorers,
> painters and journalists were sump-
> tuously received with a munificence
> never to be forgotten that left them
> almost breathless.[2]

The following description of the Qurdan manor
house, though it could more truthfully be labeled an
inventory, comes from information given to Mme
Bassenne by the widow of a cavalry officer, Colonel
Grand-Conseil, who in 1893 was a lieutenant accom-
panying his superior officer on an expedition to
Qurdan.

> Having partaken of an abundant lunch
> with a qaid en route for Qurdan, and not
> too disposed to ride, they left the
> grooms to follow with the horses while
> the officers continued the excursion by
> mule cart.
> The trail must be lovely to ride
> along, but what a difference sitting in
> the cart, nothing but bumps and jolts
> made worse by the wielding of the whip
> with which our enthusiastic black driver
> encouraged the three strong animals to
> race along at full tilt.
> Half way, at 'Ain Madi, at a spring
> tended by natives and irrigating a
> future barley crop, our driver stopped
> and pointed to a white shimmer in the
> distance . . . Qurdan at last!
> About fifteen minutes before our

38

arrival we saw coming toward us a dozen riders; they were our hosts. They arrived at a gallop and leaped from their saddles. We, too, dismounted from the cart and were introduced to Sidi 'Ali bin Ahmad Tijani, the son of the sharif, a negroid young man of about twenty who spoke French easily and fluently. After much handshaking and kisses on our respective index fingers, we got back on to our cart escorted by Sidi Ahmad's deputies.

The shaikh's son rode a magnificent light grey hose richly harnessed. The embroidered saddle was equipped with silver stirrups and the under blanket and leather breast plate was literally covered in gold thread. His own dress was that of a well-to-do local Arab, green waistcoat and baggy green pants; an immaculately white over garment and over all flowed a burnous to match the pants and waistcoat. The splendor of this outfit put the clothes of our other hosts completely in the shade--and yet they, too, were richly dressed.

On rounding the last buttress of Jabal 'Amr in a completely barren countryside, there was Qurdan. A dwelling which would have been called a castle on the other side of the Mediterranean. It was a vast house in a semi-French and semi-Arab style.

We entered a lower drawing room where we waited the mistress of the household, Mme Aurélie Tijani. She is a large, well-built woman of about forty years. [Aurelie had gained weight with time.] She wore a party dress of peacock blue velours adorned with superb jewels.

We were graciously received, then escorted up to the first floor to be introduced to the head of the order of the Tijaniya. I was expecting to see a man of great bearing, but instead I found a very fat man, wheezing and puffing, but amiable. His dress was simple, a large cashmere gandura [man's baggy dress] in a shrimp pink and a muslin turban.

39

Conversation began between him and the captains. I took a look at the scene. We were in a vast room and a single carpet covered the entire length of the floor. In the center was a table covered with a black velvet drape with gold embroidered Arabic inscriptions. Above this hung a bronze and crystal chandelier of a church style, while around the table were six Damascene chairs of the most delicate inlaid fretwork. Around the walls were more chairs and sofas inlaid with mother-of-pearl and upholstered with embroidered brocade from the Orient. Against the wall-panels spread a wonderful display of Arab and Turkish arms. Facing these was the fireplace and mantelpiece on which was a very valuable copper Syrian clock. Above this hung a beveled mirror. On either side of the chimney stood a cabinet encrusted also in mother-of-pearl and opposite these, at the other end of the room, was a very high window draped with three pairs of curtains.

We were served tea and coffee, and later, the shaikh's son took us round the property on a tour of inspection. We glanced into the stables in which there were fifty horses and thirty mules; we noticed a mill house and mud built houses for the farmers--of whom there were about two hundred--so our host informed us.

But the dinner hour was upon us; we entered a small and simple dining room supplied with a profusion of beautiful silverware, and an excellent dinner. The only complaint against it was that it was two dinners! To begin with, a French dinner of six courses, followed by an Arab dinner of six courses, from which we simply could not be excused. Our host's son supervised and it would have been rude not to have tasted everything. While we were dining our beds were prepared in the ground floor drawing room; now further decorated by two remarkable incense burners.

Next day we bade our farewells to the lord of the manor and an escort of

40

his relatives accompanied us to the
halfway point of our road to 'Ain Madi.[3]

After the death of Aurélie's father, while she
was still living at 'Ain Madi, most of her family
moved to Algeria, no doubt hoping to jump on the
rich band wagon. Aurélie considered her generosity
had gone far enough when she installed her mother in
her house in Algiers (given to her by Sidi Ahmad).
The old lady was so poor, living on a pittance of a
police pension, that she could not even afford the
help of a servant. This was bad for the colonial
image, something Aurélie should have realized. Nor
did she treat her brothers and sisters-in-law any
better. When a nephew was born she sent the parents
a coin of 20 francs as a gift--which was almost an
insult--considering her personal wealth. Aurélie
was a miser.

Aurélie constantly received incredibly valuable gifts, particularly from the Ahaggar Tuareg
members of the order who showered her with presents.
Among them was a tent in red leather, twenty meters
in diameter and completely lined in velvet. She had
it put up in the garden and often gave her guests
tea beneath this munificent example of the people's
fidelity.

Nor was it unusual for the wives of prominent
Muslim Algerians to visit her. Cold by nature, she
haughtily ordered coffee to be served when they
would probably have preferred tea. They, with
assumed respect and natural politeness, stripped
themselves of their jewelry, bracelets, gold
necklaces, jeweled pendants and earrings, throwing
them into the folds of Aurelie's lap. Her coffers
were filled with enormous quantities of gold and
silver jewelry, some of which were very old and
rare.

Only occasionally, for fun, did Aurélie dress
in Arab clothes. The flowing haik, a fine, hand-
woven length of material several meters long, caught
in at the waist gave her a very regal appearance and
regal she felt as she carried quite majestically the
weight she had gained. Even so, despite the rigors
of the climate, she was happiest in Western clothes,
which were not always in the best of taste and often
very ornate. For grand receptions she wore garish
brocades and velvet draped in lace and silks, and
covered herself with glittering jewels. On her
visits to Algiers, milliners and dressmakers cheated
her and took advantage of her ignorance of fashion
and her inability to distinguish between quiet

41

elegance and flashy gaudiness. This was a lesson
that had obviously not been learned during her youth
as a dressmaker and lady's maid. She seems to have
felt that the "correctness" of her costumes were
guaranteed if their price was high enough! Indeed,
she once created a sensation when she walked out
from her milliner wearing a hat weighed down by a
crown of life-size imitation tortoises.

Because of the difficult journey, Aurélie only
visited Algiers once every two or three years to
replenish her wardrobe and furnishings and to buy
clothes for her many servants. She no longer rode
but travelled in a carriage drawn by four strong
mules, whipped to a gallop by a black coachman. On
these occasions she would stay with her mother, but
Aurélie did not care for city life and was always in
a hurry to get back to her beautiful desert. (There
she would have a point in common with Isabelle
Eberhardt.) Outside of her family she was kind and
helpful to those in need, but quite intransigeant
about the slightest carelessness in anyone who
worked for her. Her sister-in-law recounted an
episode wherein Aurélie had bought some five hundred
burnouses as gifts for numerous countrymen and had
them put away in an empty room awaiting her
departure. Every morning this room was washed by a
number of black women, the water being mopped and
sloshed carelessly as is their way. On the day of
departure the clothes were brought out and many of
them were found to be wet, mouldy, and badly
stained. Aurélie said not a word but called the
women to her and from the folds of her clothes drew
a whip that she was never without. The unfortunate
women threw themselves at her feet crying and
begging for mercy. She ignored their pleas and with
a cold brutality whipped them till her sister-in-law
could stand it no longer. "STOP!" she screamed,
snatching at the whip. "They're human beings, for
God's sake!" Aurélie replied grimly through tight
lips, "I must teach them to respect me."[4]

Aurélie had her own troubles, both at 'Ain
Madi and at Qurdan, though she closed her eyes to
her husband's affairs and the scandals he created
with his loose and degenerate behavior at Qurdan.
Both Sidi Ahmad and Sidi al-Bashir had become
drunkards during their enforced residence in France.
'Ali, her stepson, was even more dissolute than his
father as well as being lazy and a spendthrift.

After a visit to Algiers, during which Sidi
Ahmad deeded two more houses to his wife, he was
called to 'Ain Madi, where trouble awaited. For a

long time al-Bashir had been jealous and resentful especially when his brother was away and al-Bashir was forced to ask for prior approval of his actions from his sister-in-law rather than from Sidi Ahmad. After the trip to Algiers, the two brothers quarreled constantly, Aurélie usually being the cause, until events came to a dramatic head, as related by a Zouave (NCO) who was preparing a billet for an officer stationed there.[5]

On July 5, 1882, about two thirty in the afternoon as I was on my way back from the work site, Sidi Qaddur, one of the saint's sons, rushed up to me begging me to go to Sidi Ahmad.

When I arrived on the terrace I found Sidi al-Bashir completely drunk with his feet in irons. Al-Bashir called out, "It's for me that you have been called." As I looked, taken aback, Sidi 'Ali came up to me and said "Take no notice, he's drunk, go and see my father." So I continued on my way, still accompanied by Sidi Qaddur. Al-Bashir shrieked at his son and threatened him, whereupon he took fright and ran off.

I went to see Sidi Ahmad who was with Mme Tijani, she said "Monsieur, would you please arrest Sidi al-Bashir, he is drunk and has just tried to shoot his brother. And yesterday he was in the same state and fired at one of his sons." I asked the reason why and she replied that he was drunk and didn't know what he was doing and then he started beating up one of his wives. She went to complain to Sidi Ahmad who sent for his brother and ticked him off for his behavior.

Sidi al-Bashir flew into a rage and rushed to a room where firearms were kept. Not having the keys, he bashed the door down, grabbed a double-barreled shotgun and ran back to the room where his brother was. The boys tried to stop him and he fired at them but missed. Sidi Ahmad, hearing the shot, came to the door and that was when he fired the second time. The bullet passed through his robe causing a flesh wound above the knee and lodged in the wall. He was quite berserk, hitting anyone who came near him and breaking everything within reach--we had to put him in stocks.

Mme Aurélie asked me to take him back to his quarters and put him under guard. I said I did not have the authority to do this but would get a letter off to the duty officer at Laghouat. I had barely started writing when Sidi Qaddur came to fetch me again to go to Sidi Ahmad who was frightened saying that his brother was trying to break his irons with stones . . . that his brother must be taken away, anything could happen. One of them would have to leave 'Ain Madi because if al-Bashir became drunk again he probably would succeed in killing his brother.

Sidi Ahmad had al-Bashir taken back to his house and I agreed to keep it guarded until the arrival of the duty officer. Sidi Ahmad also stated, "My brother is very jealous and whenever I give anything to the French he picks a quarrel with me." I think he was alluding this time to some land that had been given for the construction of a Bureau Arabe.

After the attempt on his brother's life Sidi al-Bashir was ordered to Tamasin on the pretext of improving relations between the two zawiyas. His arrival there was both unexpected and disagreeable; Sidi Mu'ammar bin al-Hajj 'Ali felt that al-Bashir was nothing but a troublemaker and that his brother (Sidi Ahmad) was only out for himself and did not want the responsibility of a discontented al-Bashir. In a letter to the Commandant of Laghouat dated 8 September 1882, Sidi Ahmad al-Tijani was full of excuses about how al-Bashir had had to fend for himself from a very young age and had therefore grown up unaware of his responsibilities. In order to learn these and to quieten down, said Sidi Ahmad, a spell at the Tamasin zawiya among serious and religious people would do him good. He added in the last paragraph that he considered al-Bashir incapable of rendering service to the government since he was not seriously inclined, while he, Sidi Ahmad, was ready to carry out any orders he may have been given in the general interests of the government.

44

Although Aurélie maintained her prerogatives at the 'Ain Madi zawiya, she was aware of the bitterness and hate she aroused, despite her efforts to alleviate the prevailing poverty. Life there had become more difficult, because she was living so close to al-Bashir, his wives, and old women, the concubines--including those of Sidi Ahmad--and the sons and uncles.

Since Sidi Ahmad and Mme Tijani had taken up permanent residence at Qurdan, two zawiya nuclei had formed, that in 'Ain Madi where al-Bashir had returned, and a second in Qurdan.

The pilgrims who visited the tomb of Sidi Muhammad al-Saghir passed by Qurdan to receive the hospitality of the chief of the Tijaniya--hospitality paid for by gifts more or less remunerative, by a sheep or wool, sacks of grain or jugs of butter, smin. Whatever it was and whatever its value it was gracefully accepted by the shaikh and then put to good use by his wife or carefully stored away; it was these gifts that were a shaikh's due and considerably reduced his cost of living.

To Aurélie these visits were very important; by example she was able to show the pilgrims that order and care brought forth fruitfulness with such abundance as to be worthy of Paradise. It must certainly be a miracle, they thought, that fruit and vegetables could be so succulent and plentiful. They were shown the farming implements, the judicious use of animal manure and were given a small variety of healthy seeds to take back with them to plant in their oasis plots with instructions on how to plant them. These were carefully carried deep in the hoods of the pilgrims' burnouses. They were convinced that the seeds were potent with supernatural virtue and that this was one more manifestation of the fact that the shaikh had spread his baraka even to the plants and vegetables around him. It is unlikely that in those days they associated such abundance with European know-how. In a letter to her brother Aurélie wrote:

> One day at Laghouat a villager saw in my room a bunch of flowers that I had picked. He threw himself upon them and kissed them passionately, begging that I give him just one to plant so that it could root and become a talisman--a flowering talisman. I gave him the whole bunch as it was faded and drying up. "My poor man," I said, "How do you

45

think those half dead stalks will take
root? . . . "Because they are holy
flowers and flowers from saints never
die!" He was angry and claimed that
because my infidel hands touched them,
they had annihilated the _baraka_.[6]

In addition to agricultural improvements, a
school was built for boys where they were clothed
and fed by the _zawiya_, with two aims in mind: (1)
the material well-being of the Arab family, and (2)
of great significance, Francophile educational
instruction. Aurélie was constantly pushing the
shaikh toward fresh undertakings beneficial to
France. Despite the outward successes and her
husband's renown, there was continual domestic
trouble caused by Sidi Ahmad's son, 'Ali. He was
depicted as an elegant, amiable man of the world,
but he lived an idle, indulgent life, trying to copy
European ways but unable to do so. He dressed in
expensive clothes, drank, and consorted with costly
whores. His lavish gambling at baccarat soon landed
him in the hands of Jewish money lenders.
Unfortunately many bored youths of old established
families behaved similarly, acquiring only the vices
of Westernization while losing the virtues of their
own culture. Sidi 'Ali was weak like his father,
and easily gave in to the temptations surrounding
him, allowing flattery of false friends to interfere
with his studies. It was well known that Sidi Ahmad
was so disgusted with his son that not only did he
refuse to see him, but he refused to entertain the
idea of 'Ali's becoming his successor.
        In the east, too, at Tamalhat and Gaymar, the
young shaikhs were behaving badly, so that Sidi
Mu'ammar in exasperation sent a telegram to the
colonel commanding the Biskra region requesting him
to arrest his two nephews, Muhammad al-Tahar and
Sa'id bin Khadiri, aged twenty-seven and seventeen
respectively. They frequently went to Tuggurt to
get drunk and visit the brothels and returned to the
zawiya still drunk, noisy, obstreperous and lacking
all respect for their religious elders. Both were
imprisoned for a month but to little avail. In 1892
Sa'id bin Khadiri obtained money and a travel permit
to go to Laghouat, but he never arrived as he spent
all his money in his old stomping grounds of Tuggurt
and was once again arrested by the authorities.
        These domestic worries, near and far, did not
help Sidi Ahmad, for he was very sick with diabetes
and grossly overweight. Aurélie was his sole com-

fort. In spite of the myriad of cultural differences, theirs was a happy marriage; the shaikh depended on his wife and listened to her wise counsel. Both were much attracted toward the branch zawiyas in Tunisia, and for a long time the shaikh had entertained the idea of closer relations between them, so that he could make his influence felt both then and in the future. Aurélie dearly wished she had a son, and then 'Ain Madi could be left behind to the care of the other Tijani shaikhs while she, with her son, could colonize the estates owned by the Tijaniya in Tunisia--a country of great agricultural resources.

The couple's thoughts had turned to the east and to the great zawiya of Tamasin/Tamalhat, the sly rival of 'Ain Madi. For many years the French administration had refused permission to allow Sidi Ahmad to pay it a personal visit; preferring to keep him nearer to home where they could watch him. It was only after the explosive quarrel in 1884 that Sidi al-Bashir was allowed to carry out periodic visits for diplomatic or ziyara collection purposes on behalf of his brother or close relatives, to important zawiyas or to other distant, influential chiefs affiliated with the order. During the polite visits to Tamalhat (the zawiya of Tamasin) there was an exchange of gifts and money between the two zawiyas. The saints of Tamasin particularly valued black women and slaves.

Despite their rivalry, Aurélie did her best to maintain a semblance of good relations between the two zawiyas. It was Sidi Mu'ammer, the brother of the dissident shaikh at Tamasin who was given the responsibility of the return visits to 'Ain Madi. He was an adroit and diplomatic individual with a jolly Rabelaisian sense of humor whose persuasion made Sidi Ahmad determined to visit the zawiyas in the east. He was still obsessed with the idea of going to Tunisia, hoping, through his illustrious presence, to woo the zawiyas of Tunisia to 'Ain Madi, and in so doing, to consolidate his own power and the prestige of 'Ain Madi.

The idea was right, but the timing was wrong; Sidi Ahmad was a sick man, and Aurélie begged him to postpone such a gruelling journey. But in front of this idée fixé she was powerless and finally gave in to this man who was hugely fat, diabetic and prematurely old, but whom she still loved. Arrangements went ahead, and on Christmas day in 1896 Sidi Ahmad set off in great style, his carriage pulled by several sturdy horses and whipped to the usual gallop by the black coachman. He was accompanied by his second son and by thirteen other members of the order (including five shurfa and five l-Arba' tribesmen), four black servitors and twenty-four camelmen. The itinerary of the cortege was to Gurara, Tuggurt, (and Tamasin), El Oued and Gaymar, and then on to Tawzar (Touzeur) and Nafta across the border in Tunisia, and possibly from there to Tunis and to Constantine, with the return to 'Ain Madi via Bu Sa'ada and Julfa, if his health permitted.[7] This of course presupposes that Sidi Ahmad had at last obtained clearance from the governor general in Algiers to visit Tunisia for ziyara collection. So with his retinue he drew up in front of the hotel, where General Ruyssen, commander of the region, lived, to make his farewells.

"You are making a mistake in going," said the general, who liked Sidi Ahmad. "What you are about to undertake is far too tiring for you."

"Yet I must, it is mandatory that I go," replied Sidi Ahmad obstinately. "My interests and duty call me there." The shaikh was not to be thwarted of his dream; it had taken so long to get the authority to go. The general persisted that Sidi Ahmad's interests also lay in 'Ain Madi, but the shaikh countered that nothing amiss would happen during his absence as his wife was there and all would go smoothly in her capable hands.

Full of jubilant hopes he left with his escort of members of the order and from time to time Qurdan received serene and happy letters full of the news of the welcome he was given along the route. At Tamasin, though, sickness struck: anthrax, a serious illness, and particularly so for the shaikh in his diabetic condition. Sidi Ahmad was cared for and cured sufficiently to continue his journey for a further sixty kilometers (quite a distance in 1896-97, over desert trails) as he was spurred on by his desire to become acquainted with the seven Tunisian zawiyas of the Tijaniya. So he arrived at Gaymar, near El Oued, on the Tunisian frontier, a relatively new zawiya and whose muqaddamin the shaikh greatly wanted as his allies, as a counterbalance to those of Tamalhat/Tamasin.

Once again, however, his illness broke out and now poor Sidi Ahmad realized that he had been wrong and that he could never complete his long journey. He wanted to go home in all haste, to be close to his faithful companion Aurélie, and he started a letter to her to this effect; alas, he was unable to finish it. He suffered severe complications and blood poisoning from which he never recovered, and he died on April 20, 1897.

What a godsend, however, for the muqaddamin in the east that the head of the Tijaniya should die within their region! The body of the shaikh whose baraka they had contested during his lifetime, became a priceless relic that must be kept at Gaymar, a relic that could invoke miracles and attract wealth through alms. Gaymar would benefit and the muqaddamin of eastern Algeria may even have hoped that this event would bring about a dissolution of the order at 'Ain Madi and attract its entire South Algerian membership to them. All that was needed were a few stories and legends astutely spread to turn Sidi Ahmad's death into a miracle and ruin the faith in the descendants of the founder still within the cradle of the order.

Sadness and consternation reigned in 'Ain Madi and Qurdan. The notables of the muqaddamin met in a hadra, reunion, and in accordance with the Sidi Ahmad's wishes, his son Sidi 'Ali was bypassed as the next candidate, and his brother, al-Bashir, was named as the next head of the Tijaniya. Whereupon, following Aurélie's orders, al-Bashir set off to Gaymar to bring back his brother's remains. This was to cause a drama and an inter-zawiya quarrel of major proportions: for it is standard practice for any Muslim to be buried where he dies, and as soon after death as possible. Aurélie, in trying to alter this procedure and have Sidi Ahmad's body exhumed was most certainly contravening custom and practice.

Once this project became known there was a general outcry from the muqaddamin in the east. They protested to the administration against removing the body and whipped up the members of the order in the oases of the Suf about it. When the new shaikh arrived from 'Ain Madi, he found himself among a hostile and threatening community who appeared determined to oppose him, by force, if necessary. In 1897, after all, a journey from 'Ain Madi to Gaymar was not done in just a few days, and Sidi Ahmad had been buried for quite a while.

Mme Aurélie Tijani, in the midst of her grief and the uncertainties in which she found herself, never neglected the Tijaniya interests. Although she had never openly asked for active help in France (though she must have received it financially, as her considerable wealth did not accrue from the coffers of the Tijaniya of 'Ain Madi) she did so now. While Sidi al-Bashir was away, Aurélie paid a visit to General Ruyssen, putting forth her point of view. Had not 'Ain Madi and the Tijani family worked hard enough for France to merit its protection and justice? How could Sidi Ahmad after his death bring saintliness to a distant zawiya with which he had always quarreled during his lifetime? And did not Aurélie herself have every right to the mortal remains of a husband whom she had loved and helped for over twenty-five years?

She took the matter even further up the chain of command, to the governor general of Algeria, and the correspondence, via General Ruyssen and other military commanders, both in the Algerois and Constantinois departments, was copious and acrimonious.[8] The French were between the muqaddamin in the east and Mme Tijani of Qurdan, both of whom they wanted to placate. In the interim, Sidi al-Bashir was no match for the muqaddamin at Gaymar, and he returned empty-handed, to Aurélie's fury. Not only had he been unable to impose his will as the chief of the Tijaniya, but the cunning muqaddam of Tamasin and Gaymar had further wrung an agreement from him that he would leave the dead shaikh's body there as a sign of his good faith.

The weak-willed shaikh was in bad odor with Mme Tijani, and she refused to even consider his backing down, forcefully continuing to push her claim to her husband's precious body and prodding the Tijaniya with all the authority she possessed to join in the struggle against their brothers in the east.

Lengthy correspondence ensued between the authorities, 'Ain Madi, and the eastern zawiyas; Sidi Ahmad's escort wanted to return immediately with his body but, as Sidi Muhammad al-'Arusi pointed out to the French commandant, this would be unhygienic in the early summer heat. He also noted that it was against all the principles and traditions of the founders of the order, and in fact of those of Islam in general, to exhume the body. He knew perfectly well that Mme Tijani was behind it all and that she should mind her own business; it was entirely a religious affair, quite apart from the fact that Sidi Ahmad was buried next to his sisters. The see-saw fight continued for many weeks. Al-'Arusi wrote to Sidi al-Bashir himself saying that his brother had already been buried for fifty days and, given the rudimentary means of transport, exhumation would be both unsanitary and unpleasant. Al-'Arusi bluntly stated, furthermore, that such an act would be unpardonable in the eyes of God and His Prophet, and that he, al-Bashir, would be remembered for generations for such despicable behavior.

> We beg you my lord, to abandon your project as it can only weaken your standing and dignity with the order. We can only ask you to ask God to help you face whoever is the instigator of this idea. Your grandfather died in Fez, his tomb was respected by Sidi al-Hajj 'Ali who only brought back his children. We pray to God to make you beware of your short-sightedness and go back on your idea. That your arrival here will only render homage to your brother and in so doing God will forgive all the bad that is being said of you.[9]

Al-Bashir wanted nothing more than to conform with custom and tradition and to be rid of Aurélie and her blatant disregard for Islamic traditions.

Even al-Bashir's close kinswomen wrote to Aurelie. But she paid short shrift to them, stating that her claim was backed by the authority of the Supreme Shaikh of the order, and God's representative of it on earth. She cared not one iota for their feelings of outrage and further strengthened her demands by pointing out that a shrine had already been built in the garden of Qurdan and that this was the logical place for her husband to rest. Why should the faithful fill another's coffers with their offerings (ziyarat) when she considered herself to be the rightful heir?

Other interviews between al-Bashir and the authorities further reveal his indecisive character, for he was now claiming that he had made a firm agreement with the shaikh at Gaymar to leave the body there. He claimed that whatever had been agreed upon had been under duress and the angry threats of the muqaddam. For her part, Aurélie upbraided her brother-in-law continually, finally threatening him that if he did not bring Sidi Ahmad's body back from Gaymar she would leave the country and never return. This dire threat and the consequence it would have had for him finally broke down his misgivings. He was in any case putty in her hands, and she had a greater dominance over him than over her late husband.

To bring the bickering to an end, the governor general, Louis Lepine, demanded a personal interview with Mme Tijani and promised her French support in the following words: "I assure you, Madame, that the body of Sidi Ahmad will be returned to 'Ain Madi, but it is out of consideration for you that I am authorizing this restitution; for Sidi al-Bashir, who did not know how to effect this matter in Gaymar, does not deserve it." Sidi al-Bashir was, of course, torn between religious tradition, Aurélie, and his subservience to the French. General Déchizelle, who commanded the Batna section of the Division of Constantine and had not a good word to say for Aurélie, was forced by orders from above to give his consent to the exhumation. "We would only alienate Sidi al-Bashir who seems well disposed to serve us as well as displeasing Mme Aurélie by a contrary decision which would surely bring about her departure. This would be a very grave political error with unforeseeable consequences."[10]

Aurélie knew she had everyone over a barrel. The authorization having come through, Sidi al-Bashir was free to leave. Such journeys though, for people of consequence, were long, slow, and dignified. Military communication, on the other hand, was relatively fast. So in the interim of January 1898, General Fontebride, commanding the subdivision of Batna wrote a strongly worded letter to the general commanding the Division of Constantine:

> The possession of two hundred camels that are accompanying Sidi al-Bashir leaves no doubt in anybody's minds of the pomp in which he (al-Bashir) plans to travel to Gaymar. However, in view of the great poverty of our natives I would be most obliged if you would strictly forbid Sidi al-Bashir from collection of any ziyara in the territory of the command of Tuggurt. The marabout and his late brother have already received large amounts of ziyara during their last journey through this particular territory.[11]

It was in November 1897 that Sidi al-Bashir set out with his cortege, further strengthened by a detachment of artillery for his protection and to enforce the orders from Algiers, if necessary; and it was early in February 1898, when the travellers eventually arrived at Gaymar.

Sidi Ahmad's body had been laid in a zinclined wooden coffin in a vault between his sister and a son of Sidi al-Hajj 'Ali. The two latter had been dead for about fifteen years, and, as their coffins were almost completely rotten, they had been removed with great difficulty to make room for Sidi Ahmad. It was no easy task to bring up the late shaikh's casket as he had been excessively corpulent at the time of his death. Finally, however, at 10 p.m., on 10 February 1898, Sidi Ahmad's body was exhumed and began its return journey. The coffin hung between two mules and, accompanied by his pious followers, travelled across the South Algerian Desert. It was a venerated object for the tribes that were met along the way and, again, the journey lasted several weeks.

When the cortege arrived at the outer limits of Mme Tijani's domain its precious cargo was transferred to a rough catafalque round which were gathered the family and the faithful of the Tijaniya. The night was filled with their weeping and lamentations, and prayers echoed across the desert and silent dunes. Sidi Ahmad's last resting place was in a colonnaded pink marble qubba (shrine with a cupola) which Aurélie had built in the garden of Qurdan beneath the ancient fig tree.

To show the establishment's esteem for Sidi Ahmad, a religious sermon and prayers were held in Algiers in the Turkish-built Hanafi mosque. This mosque is properly named Jami' al-Jadid, the new Mosque, but the French, with a complete and colonial disregard for Arabic and Islam, labeled it "La Mosquée des Pêcheurs". The ceremony was attended by a number of Frenchmen. The new governor, Jules Cambon, spoke in his funeral eulogy about Sidi Ahmad having been a true friend of France and further stated: "He served civilization, [France] by his example and prepared the way for her." This was neatly put, for France already had her eyes on Morocco and Tunisia. Aurélie had worn the pants in the family; Sidi Ahmad had been very largely her tool; and her identification with French interests was total.

However, as has been made clear earlier, Sidi Ahmad, far from breaking with Tijaniya tradition in his collaboration with the French, had merely retrenched and underlined the position of the order as a whole in Algeria: for in its insistence on its members making pilgrimages exclusively to the tomb of its founder, Sidi Ahmad al-Tijani the Elder, it had already broken with the North African Muslim tradition of diffuse saint worship, even before the

French arrived. Its aim was a more universalistic Islam, and it saw collaboration with a colonial power as the best way of achieving this objective. In this sense, the open and avowed collaboration of Sidi Ahmad Tijani the younger need not be regarded entirely pejoratively. Indeed, a thread of early reformism is quite discernible, even if it seems mild by comparison with early twentieth century Islamic reforms and the fundamentalism of today.

Chapter 5

MARRIAGE TO SIDI AL-BASHIR TIJANI (1898-1911)
AND THE AFTERMATH (1911-1933)

Sidi Ahmad's death left a void in Aurélie's
life. Once the last respects had been paid, she
assumed that her role in his Algerian Muslim family
would be at an end and that she would have to return
to Algiers to live out the rest of her years in
retirement. But Sidi al-Bashir, left to his own
devices in running the zawiya, was dismayed at the
enormity of his responsibilities, and the order's
notables did not really want to see her gone from
them. No doubt they sowed the idea in Sidi
al-Bashir's mind to marry his brother's widow; for
widow inheritance is institutionalized in Islam as a
means to keep property within the family, as well as
to provide for a bereaved widow.

Rumors of a possible marriage soon reached
General Collet-Meygret, the commander of the
Division of Algiers, who approved the union,
figuring there was still a great deal Aurélie could
do for the colonial administration. He also agreed
with the shaikhs of 'Ain Madi on the advantages of
having Mme Tijani maintain her accustomed place so
that nothing would change in the administration of
the zawiya.[1] Al-Bashir's loss of religious prestige
during the affair at Gaymar made the shaikhs even
more concerned with maintaining administrative
continuity. However, in a traditional Muslim
society such as that at 'Ain Madi, Mme Tijani--a
childless widow--would have had no place; nor could
she have lived alone on the estate she had created.
It is true that the local Arabs had become used to
seeing her in command, but always alongside her
husband.

The idea of marriage was abhorrent to the
prospective participants, whose mutual animosity had
increased since the furious argument between the
brothers which ended in drunken shots and al-Bashir
in irons. The personal hatred between Aurélie and
Sidi al-Bashir highlighted the quarrel within the

55

brotherhood (Appendix B). However, during Aurelie's absence from Laghouat and the acrimonious bickering over the patronymic, standards of agriculture at 'Ain Madi and Qurdan had rapidly disintegrated. Sidi al-Bashir was quite incapable of managing Qurdan or even 'Ain Madi on his own. So Mme Tijani, acknowledging that her political and economic obligations were still unfinished, agreed to marry al-Bashir.

Aurélie could not abandon twenty-five years of her life's work nor the respect she had gained. At Qurdan she had become a personage in her own right, and, in effect, had such delusions of grandeur as to insist that everyone bow before her, even members of her own family, and that an Arab should kiss the hem of her robes before addressing her! Aurélie was already planning new ways to use her established power and to tear further riches from the barren territory which she was already exploiting. The return journey south was not nearly as arduous as had been her first one, for she was now able to travel the first hundred miles by train. Therefore, she took her mother with her for a visit, regretting only that her father, an old French <u>vieux-moustache</u> of Algeria and now dead, could not have seen her wealth.

On arrival, Aurélie informed Sidi al-Bashir that she would consent to the marriage. Thus a year after widowhood she and Sidi al-Bashir were married in front of the qadi at Laghouat. It was a legal Muslim marriage. She had not forgotten the outrage, the slights, and the refusal of the military administration to consent to a civil union for her first marriage. And so she had a certain satisfaction and revenge in refusing in her turn the French civil ceremony that was now offered for her second wedding.

Despite the splendor of the marriage ritual-- the drums, and dancing, and the feasting befitting the new Tijani leader--it was entirely a marriage of convenience, existing only in the register. Once the ceremonies were over, Aurélie returned to Qurdan and Sidi al-Bashir went back to his other two wives living in the carefree dilapidation of 'Ain Madi.

Life once more became, or at least seemed, as brilliant as it had been in the past. The prosperity of Qurdan was at its apogee and Aurélie, now completely at ease, enjoyed to the full the authority, fortune, and glory she had imagined thirty years ago. The relationship of the couple was limited to interviews necessitated by the management of the zawiya. Frequently, Aurélie just let her decisions be known to her husband by a messenger; the only usefulness her name of Tijani now had was for official functions and receptions. Even so, Aurélie had to tread with care with regard to 'Ain Madi where some still hated her. Al-Bashir could easily be swayed by shaikhs hostile to her and to the French administration. She feared for the welfare of her beloved Qurdan for another reason: since Sidi Ahmad's death his son, Sidi 'Ali, had begun to work actively against her and to undermine her authority. While the Tijaniya zawiyas in Algeria were backed by the French, other religious orders resented greatly the growing colonization of their lands and of the country at large. Since there was no closeness between the married couple, physical or spiritual, and as Sidi al-Bashir was the supreme shaikh with all the authority his position carried, Aurélie very definitely had to give up any ideas she might have entertained of collaboration with the White Fathers, and ultimately of attempting to implant Christianity in the country--a project that had been close to Cardinal Lavigerie's heart when he originally married Aurélie Picard to Sidi Ahmad al-Tijani in 1871.

It was still a brilliant period for Aurélie; she was now a woman in her fifties, very sure of herself and her standing with the French. According to a description by Soleillet, the explorer, in 1872, she was no longer a slight young woman, but, being tall, her added weight lent dignity to her figure. She was indifferent to and out of touch with fashion and still wore dresses of the Second Empire era, but who would dare laugh about such things in Aurélie's presence? Colonial and officers' wives never left the Tell, and the Muslim ladies of her entourage who wore traditional Algerian dress had every reason to take Aurélie's clothes to be "traditional" French attire.

From a feminine point of view, the accounts of neither Mmes Bassenne nor Crosnier made mention of how Mme Tijani fared when she mixed with her compatriots at receptions and official functions in Algiers (the journey there and back having become progressively easier). Fashions had greatly changed by the early 1900's, but Aurélie always wore full evening regalia, resplendent with jewels, whatever the occasion, so she must have been a "character," though an intimidating one. Surely some of the ladies of French Algerian society, however much they snickered, must have admired Aurélie's courage and

57

audacious tenacity in the face of a lonely and hard desert life.

In 1903, when the President of the Republic visited Algiers, Mme Tijani was awarded the Order of Merit for Agriculture, and in 1906 she was named an Officer of the Academy for having created several schools from personal funds. She had, in fact, built four separate schools for boys and girls and one in particular in 'Ain Madi where the village girls could learn sewing, weaving, hygiene, and the rudiments of formal instruction in French.

In 1911, when General Jean Bailloud, who commanded the nineteenth Army Corps in Algiers, visited Qurdan shortly after Sidi al-Bashir had become a Chevalier of the Legion of Honor, he was astonished to learn that Aurélie had not received the same honor. He made the following remark to a colleague: "After fifty years of effort to achieve some semblance of civilization <u>alone</u> in a harsh, burning desert climate, Mme Tijani never abandoned her French personality and way of life. Although she brought profits and benefits to an important Muslim Algerian order and almost finished up as being their chief, she still remained a Christian."[2] A very colonial comment one might say, today, but Aurélie no doubt had spunk and drive, and certainly around Qurdan she was loved and revered almost as a saint.

If Shaikh Sidi al-Bashir al-Tijani was worthy of the red ribbon (and, in truth, he was the laziest shaikh of the brotherhood), Aurélie Tijani no doubt merited it considerably more. In fact, both Sidi Ahmad and Sidi al-Bashir had been ill-prepared for their roles. Their intrigues made them at times very difficult to deal with, but, due to Aurelie's foresighted diplomacy, they became devout and firm backers of the French administration.

General Bailloud promised to do what he could to obtain the Legion of Honor for Mme Tijani. But with World War I on the horizon and with further consolidation of the Présence Française in Algeria, the request for such an honor and recognition was almost certainly mislaid in some files, for Aurélie was not to receive it in her lifetime.

Qurdan, however, never ceased to flourish, and Aurélie put her heart and soul into trying to instill the idea that girls, too, needed a modicum of education if only in home and infant hygiene. She was hard, she was "<u>Madame la Caisse</u>," and she was out for herself; but there are few people, even today, who can live as rough a life as she did and

58

still achieve what she achieved alone. Even American pioneers going west in covered wagons generally traveled and toiled as families and in congenial groups and belonged to the same faith.

Aurélie was again destined to look after a mortally sick husband. Sidi al-Bashir suffered a stroke which paralyzed him, so she had him brought to Qurdan for treatment with an electrical apparatus brought specially from Algiers: one can only suppose that the electricity was supplied by a generator. A lifelong animosity laid aside, Aurélie was totally caught up in trying to restore the health of her second husband. She was probably unaware of the intrigues going on among the claimants to the baraka and the succession to the appointment of top shaikh.

As Aurélie knew, Sidi Ahmad had vehemently vetoed his son, Sidi 'Ali, as top shaikh because he was considered too dissolute to hold such an honorable position; yet now, because her second husband had not nominated a successor, she was powerless to prevent Sidi 'Ali's appointment. Sidi 'Ali was next in line agewise, in a series of successions which in 'Ain Madi had up to now favored the eldest available candidate. After further bouts of apoplectic fits, Sidi al-Bashir died of another stroke on 9 June 1911, without, unfortunately, naming a successor. The hadra, or council, of elders of the order, elected Sidi 'Ali bin Ahmad al-Tijani as supreme chief of the order, and Sidi al-Bashir was buried at 'Ain Madi next to his father and grandfather.

Was it possible that Sidi 'Ali appeared to the Tijani elders a wiser and soberer man than he had been earlier, or was it through insinuation and flattery cultivated over a long period that he was able to gather round him a circle of devoted followers? The archives do not say, and the French were not present at the deliberations on the choice of chief. That Sidi 'Ali should be named in preference to one of al-Bashir's sons, however, spelled the end of Aurélie's power. Her days at Qurdan were over; she foresaw that the management of the affairs, finances, and inheritance of the zawiya would be very different from when she had control. So she decided to leave for Algiers once her own affairs and possessions had been sorted and packed.

Two days later a French officer ordered the reading of Sidi al-Bashir's will.[3] It was not in Aurélie's favor and was greatly contested. The officer advised Aurélie to avoid trying the family too much, advice which fell on deaf ears. Her relationship with her stepson was bad, and he had no

desire to please her in any way. Other members of
the family just wanted to get rid of Aurélie as fast
as possible and prevailed upon Sidi 'Ali to let her
take what she wanted and go. Trying to be nice to
her, Sidi al-Bashir's sons said: "Take what you
want, 'mother,'" to which she replied in a hard
voice: "It's mine, anyway." In money alone they
each gave her 25,000 francs, a vast sum at the time.

Meticulously, she went through room after room
indicating what was to be packed: she pointed to the
mother-of-pearl encrusted chests, escritoires and
tables as though they belonged to her; they, too,
were allowed to go. All this was from 'Ain Madi
which had never been hers. Then Aurélie took down
all the curtains, the gold embroidered cushions, the
pictures and photographs as well as other paintings
and vases. In al-Bashir's bedroom, which had also
been Sidi Ahmad's, she left only the clothes, taking
all other personal objects, including a watch set
with precious stones and diamonds which had been a
present from the Bey of Tunis. At this point Sidi
'Ali could contain himself no longer: "Leave us
something that belongs to our family, a few carpets
and some furniture!" But even this she refused.
Why the French officer did not intervene is not
mentioned in the archival documents, which only list
her haul and tell of her hard, unfeeling attitude,
magnified no doubt because Sidi 'Ali had turned so
completely against her since his father's death.

Sidi Muhammad al-Kabir and Sidi Mahmud left
the room with tears in their eyes while Aurélie took
other watches and Sidi al-Bashir's decorations. She
even helped herself to five silver ornamented
flintlocks, only one of which had belonged to Sidi
Ahmad. The angry, silent group moved down into the
maids' room where several trunks were already
packed, locked and addressed to her brother-in-law,
Paul Keller. She said the contents of the trunks
were her younger sister's property.

"Then put them in your room," said Sidi 'Ali
grimly, "and later we'll see what is inside, in case
there should be any misunderstanding." But in the
end he let it go as he felt too sore and sick at
heart. All through the afternoon Mme Tijani continued to have things crated up. Later in the
presence of his cousins, Sidi 'Ali asked if she had
taken any money belonging to the zawiya. In fact,
he asked several times and each time she answered
"No"; they did not believe her but could not insist
and thus it was never known whether she took zawiya
money or not.

Finally, when she had taken all she wanted, which was almost everything, and when the agreement was signed, Aurélie brought up the fact that there was still owing to her 2,000 francs, her dowry from Sidi Ahmad and 1,000 francs, from Sidi al-Bashir, her second dowry. Such a claim astounded Sidi 'Ali and his cousins. They rightly and hotly objected, pointing out that Sidi Ahmad had been dead fifteen years! They asked that she produce her marriage certificates and receipts that such money had, in fact, been paid to her. She was persuaded by a mediating local notable to withdraw her claim.

Despite the shaikhs' overwhelming generosity, Aurélie's last gesture and continual complaints were despicable. As will be remembered, Mme Tijani arrived a penniless bride with no personal fortune or dowry. The fortune which she amassed over the years in money and possessions belonged to the zawiya as Ziyara donations collected and accrued through her able management, it is true, but she had no right to touch a penny of it or remove a single item.

The officer appointed to keep control of the situation, apart from being thoroughly embarrassed, was worried for Aurélie's safety. She had alienated the shaikhs and elders and all their entourage, and he was anxious to get her away as fast as possible. But there were several days of delay while Aurélie became even more exigent, bitter and vengeful. To this unfortunate officer she gave vent to feelings that she should have had her fair share of all al-Bashir's fortune; that she also had rights to Qurdan (much more to the point!), and that all the live-stock, sheep, and camels were her personal property. "It is an indignity to have named 'Ali as head of the Tijaniya . . . he is nothing but a drunkard!" Aurélie raved furiously. She stormed off to sit down and enumerate her complaints in writing to the governor general.

After almost fifty years in Algeria, closely associated with Islam and the Tijaniya order, Aurélie was, supposedly, moderately well versed in Qur'anic law and should have known that a widow only inherits one-eighth of her husband's (or husbands') property other than her dowry and personal effects which are hers for life. In the light of this, the totally egotistical fuss that she made over the whole issue seems incredible; it also seems highly colonial in that the supervising officer did nothing to restrain Aurélie or back the qadis' just protestations.

61

Finally, on 18 June 1911, at 11 a.m., Mme Tijani left Qurdan, seen off only by Sidi Mahmud and a few servants. She never expected to see the jewel of Qurdan again, and if she felt a sadness or shed a tear no one was aware of it. She asked the officer in charge to accompany her, but he declined, saying he had no orders to do so; in fact he had been told to stay in Qurdan until after her departure to ensure that there would be no harm to Aurélie from the incensed shaikhs and other members of the order.

Brazenly, and in full view of many, albeit hidden eyes, Mme Aurélie Tijani drove away with a convoy of several wagons loaded with furniture, carpets, pictures, and art treasures. During her first marriage she had never dreamed that one day she would become the wife of her detested brother-in-law, and, when many years earlier she saw Sidi Ahmad failing, she knew that, as a Christian, she would count for nothing among the Tijaniya elders and would find herself abandoned once he died. With her usual foresight, she had had Sidi Ahmad legally deed her the houses he owned in Algiers. As mentioned earlier, this had been a major bone of contention between the brothers, since al-Bashir felt that too much was going out of _zawiya_ funds for Aurélie's benefit.

However, Mme Tijani was not quite finished; she had great respect for the hazards of the future, so shortly after her arrival in Algiers, in the presence of the governor general, General Charles Lutaud, and members of the Tijani family, a formal document was signed that the sheep, camels and other livestock of Qurdan were to remain her property.

Aurélie Picard now lived close to her family in Algiers, and she also had a brother-in-law who lived in Sidi-bel-Abbes; but she lived quietly despite her fortune. She spent the years of World War I in Algiers but still contrived to have much to do with Tijani affairs.

Just before the French occupation of Morocco, Aurélie acted on her own initiative to send Tijani emissaries on journeys with propaganda favorable to the French. The continual stream of these emissaries to the Moroccan Tijaniya helped maintain their friendly and pro-French attitude, and this was invaluable when the southern oases of Morocco were captured, especially in light of the otherwise almost universal anti-French feelings of the Moroccans.

Though Mme Tijani no longer lived at Qurdan, she still kept an eye on her material interests there. She also spent considerable time visiting and rebuilding her popularity among the local Arabs which could be put to good use once again in the service of France. Lutaud, the governor general, on an official visit to the southern territories stayed at the "castle" of Qurdan (as it was then called), and on his return asked Aurélie to insist that the Tijaniya shurfa encourage enrollment of young Arabs into the French army.

Muslim Algeria heard the call of France, and a regiment of spahis (cavalry soldiers) was formed immediately; Mme Aurélie was proud of them, as well she might be; for, apart from their magnificent and colorful uniforms with their billowing capes, they were fierce warriors. Victory in Europe was what was important at the moment, and she did not wish to dwell on the fact that the men had been torn from the land which would suffer in consequence; she knew that in France other men were also leaving their own lands to lie fallow, abandoning the plow to take up the sword. As Qurdan became in need of repair she suggested to her stepson, Sidi 'Ali, that repairs undertaken early would save onerous and costly work later, but her suggestion was ignored. Sidi 'Ali was an indolent man who preferred the pleasures of Algiers, and it was not Aurélie's place to criticize the growing decay and, even less, the mismanagement of zawiya affairs.

During or after World War I, Aurélie's mother died and, with nothing much to do, Aurélie felt lonely and found that she could not adapt to city life, so, in 1920 she suddenly decided to sell her villas in Algiers and go back to France with her sister-in-law and brother to end her days in arc-en Barrois, the village of her youth.

Before leaving Algeria where she had lived for fifty years, she went to Blida to say goodbye to a brother and sister-in-law, who taught school there. From them she learnt that Sidi 'Ali was there, searching for a cure for the terrible disease that had struck him--cancer of the tongue.

What a cruel punishment from Allah on him who was so adept with words and flattery! The harsh quarrels between Aurélie and her stepson were instantly forgotten, and she was filled with grief and pity. Apart from his terrible and terminal affliction she saw immediately that he was also dying of starvation, being quite unable to swallow anything his cook made him. Aurélie took charge of the kitchen and, for the third time in her life, looked after yet another dying shaikh. She fed him

63

gently and frequently with eggs beaten to a froth
with cream--anything nourishing that could slide
painlessly down his throat. But she could not stay
indefinitely to nurse him and so instructed his cook
to carry on in the same way. With no drugs to
soothe his torment Sidi 'Ali died on 9 September
1920, and Sidi Muhammad al-Kabir bin al-Bashir, Sidi
al-Bashir's eldest son, now became the top shaikh of
the Tijaniya, continuing the established tradition
that the eldest surviving son of either of the
brothers was next in line at 'Ain Madi. Mme Tijani
was already in France when the death of her stepson
occurred.

        Although Aurélie had never forgotten the
poverty of her childhood, she had quite forgotten
how grey the skies of northern France could be, and
how the bitter cold and damp crept into the houses
and aging bones. But greater still was the shock of
Europe of the 1920's; skirts were above the knee,
and Aurélie--not having lived in wartime Europe--had
not seen and adapted herself psychologically to
their shortening. Her illusions of France and the
graciousness of life of fifty years earlier were all
rudely torn away. The shock of emancipation and
raucous music was too much for Aurélie, to say
nothing of the climate. The sun of North Africa and
its gentler pace of life was in her blood; she
longed and wished for Algeria, and, again her wish
was granted: she received an unexpected request to
return. With joy in her heart she wasted no time in
complying.[4]

2. 'Ain Madi, entrance to Tijaniya mosque, 1977.
(courtesy Donald H. Holsinger)

3. Qurdan, 1977. (courtesy Donald H. Holsinger)

4. Headstone of Aurélie Picard, 1977.
   (courtesy Donald H. Holsinger)

Chapter 6

QURDAN AGAIN AND AURÉLIE'S LAST FEW YEARS

In his lifetime Shaikh Sidi 'Ali had been an extremely docile tool in the hands of the French administration; like his father and paternal uncle, he facilitated their every move toward expansion. But his administration as seen by the Tijaniya left a great deal to be desired. His extravagance was outrageous; he indulged his every whim, buying cars as soon as they appeared in the market, and he lived in unparalleled luxury.

Sidi 'Ali soon left Qurdan to live on a property he had bought at Laghouat and which was more in line with his tastes. The absence of a leader at 'Ain Madi caused a noticeable decline among the Tijaniya.[1]

On Sidi 'Ali's death, his cousin Sidi Muhammad al-Kabir was named supreme shaikh of the Tijaniya without any opposition. But things fell apart when the heirs of the late shaikh came to divide up their possessions. The complete disorder in the zawiya administration led to bitter arguments between Sidi Muhammad, his younger brother Sidi Mahmud, and other relatives. Sidi Mahmud had gone to Fez in 1911 to try to instill loyalty toward French interests among the members of the order there. After the establishment of the Moroccan Protectorate in 1912, the French sent him on a southern tour and awarded him the Legion of Honor, but his position there became so precarious because of anti-French feelings that the authorities dared not send him back to Algeria via the southern route. Although the French authorities could meddle in the succession and inheritance only with care, they did have to intervene on occasions when dissension became violent and threatened to explode into an intra-order war.

Then, toward the end of 1922 in the middle of this turmoil which had gone on for two years and was threatening the livelihood of the 'Ain Madi zawiya, Mme Aurélie appeared most unexpectedly at Laghouat.

65

Had she been sent for by one of the other parties
who had grafted themselves on to 'Ain Madi or by the
French? The question remains open. Mme Tijani
stayed with Sidi Muhammad but also went to visit
Sidi Mahmud who had arrived by a devious route in
all haste from Morocco. She tried to remain
impartial toward the brothers, but, in reality, she
was on the side of Sidi Muhammad, whom she had
almost brought up since he was a child, and to whom
she had taught French. Aurélie had never known Sidi
Mahmud well because he had lived far away in his
mother's country.

It is certain that Aurélie was delighted at
the chance to help the zawiya. It is difficult to
discover what she actually did; the ancient walls
were thick enough to prevent eavesdropping, and Mme
Aurelie was herself far too discreet to talk, but it
can be presumed that through her calm intervention,
the succession and inheritance were arranged and the
quarrel patched up, while Aurélie was now treated
with the greatest of respect--almost with holy
reverence--by the shurfa of the Tijaniya.

Aurélie Tijani now had troubles of her own.
During her sojourn in France she probably did not
live lavishly, but she lived comfortably enough to
unwittingly draw the attention of the Inland
Revenue. A considerable amount of correspondence
passed between Aurélie and the governor general's
staff. They claimed that she was a Frenchwoman and
thus had to pay taxes on the wealth she had
acquired, including the houses she had sold in
Algiers though they had been deeded over to her
before the turn of the century!

The Inland Revenue (Overseas Department)
helpfully pointed out that it was early in 1912 that
her property had been separated from that of 'Ain
Madi and Laghouat, thus becoming French property in
French hands, and: therefore she owed them back
taxes as from the year 1912. They awaited payment.
Although Aurélie pointed out that her property was
inherited while she was resident outside France from
Muslim husbands who also lived outside France, the
Inland Revenue Bureau determined that Mme Tijani was
a French citizen and thus subject to taxation. In
the end, she had to pay ten years of taxes.

Aurélie never went back to France; she was
French but Algeria was her country. Now in her
eighties she was beginning to feel her age, and was
saddened at seeing how quickly all that she had
worked for was falling into disrepair through
laziness and indifference. Once more grasping hands

were grabbing from the till, and the rich cared nothing for the poor. Aurélie spent her time between Laghouat and the home of her nephew at Sidi-bel-Abbes. The best of her wealth in carpets, furniture, and other valuables had been carried off to France and were thus unattainable when she most needed them for the cash value they represented. It is ironic that after a life of riches and plenty, poverty was staring her in the face as she reached her last days. Pride would not allow her to ask for help from the Tijaniya. It was painful enough accepting their hospitality where she had once been mistress over everything. Finally, the French government took pity on her and, in recognition of services rendered, gave her a small pension.

Now all Mme Tijani had was a small room in one of the Tijaniya houses in Laghouat, furnished only with an iron bedstead, a table, and an old armchair. Its only ornament was a statuette on the mantelpiece. She had to sell what she had kept of her jewelry and the few other treasures to make ends meet. And it was there, in that poor and humble room, that people came to visit her. Her abrasive and forthright nature had softened with age, and it was said that during the last few years of her life people (Algerians) came to look on her almost as a saint. Maybe her simple, spartan life drew her closer to them.

On one of Aurélie's visits to Sidi-bel-Abbès, an urgent message arrived calling for her help. Qurdan was on the point of ruin, and they needed her to pull them out of their dire financial tangle. Aurélie pondered long on their predicament; she felt lethargic, her mind was hazy, and she was reluctant to make the long journey. But then was not Qurdan her dream child? It had been the scene of happiness with a husband now long dead . . . and days of glory too: she must try to save it. Aurélie mustered her diminishing forces and returned for the last time.

As she suspected, the financial depredations were too great to remedy in the time left to her; nor was there any husband to provide the incentive and awaken her business acumen. But, despite the sadness she felt at the dilapidation, Aurélie was happy to be back.

In March 1933 she became ill and was taken to the native clinic at Laghouat where the White Sisters nursed her. In August she became worse and called for Father Py to hear her last confession. When he left her bedside she called faintly for her doctor and begged him to let her return to Qurdan.

Such a move would be fatal, but how could he refuse? So he agreed to her last request, and Aurelie was happy knowing that she would be close to Sidi Ahmad, lying beneath the old, shady tree under which they had whiled away the burning summer hours when they were young and Qurdan was no more than an idea. And so it was. On Monday, 28 August 1933, Mme Aurélie Picard Tijani drew her last breath. She was buried according to her wishes in Muslim soil beside Sidi Ahmad whom she had loved.

The Tijaniya all claimed that she died a Muslim, having made the shahada, the Muslim profession of faith, a few months earlier. The White Fathers said she remained a Catholic to the end and that when she was buried she still wore the small medallion of her First Communion round her neck. Her ultimate allegiance is an enigma that remains unsolved, and the present author has no comment other than the obvious inference that throughout her life her orientations and lifestyle were far more those of a French Christian than an Algerian Muslim.

On Aurélie's last and dying journey to Qurdan in August 1933, Commandant Chaumont-Morlière awarded her the country's greatest honor and made her a Chevalier of the Legion of Honor. The citations by the Commandant are as follows:

> She reorganized and directed during forty years of her life the zawiya of Qurdan, where all the needy, sick and ailing were helped and sheltered.
> Officier du Merite Agricole
> Officier d'Academie
> Officier du Wisam al-Iftikhar [or Medal of Merit, an Algerian Decoration].
> Through her union with Sidi Ahmad she began to direct him in the service in the cause of France.
> Her directives and astute promptings allowed her brother-in-law to go to Tunisia in 1879 and to rally together members of the Tijaniya in favor of France.
> From 1881-1883 she sent envoys to Sudan on favorable propaganda missions for France toward French occupation.
> In 1896-7 she sent letters of recommendation through Sidi Ahmad to the areas where Fourneau-Lamy Mission operated.
> At the beginning of the French occu-

pation of Morocco, through emissaries sent by her second husband--through her persistent propaganda in favor of France she rendered exceptional services.

As the only Frenchwoman she isolated herself for fifty years in an important desert <u>zawiya</u>.[2]

After these posthumous citations, Commandant Chaumont-Morlière continued with a moving eulogy. A few days later a memorial service was held in Laghouat Cathedral presided over by the Bishop of the Sahara and attended by administrative officials, military personnel and other holders of the Legion of Honor who held draped between them the Death Flag of Honor.

The Tijaniya, in Algerian Muslim fashion, outlined her grave in white marble with head and foot stones as they would for one of their own venerated people. A simple inscription is written on both stones, on one side in Arabic and on the other in French.

CI GIT

MADAME AURÉLIE TIJANI

Decedee

le 28 août 1933

à l'âge de 84 ans

HERE LIES

MADAME AURÉLIE TIJANI

died

28 August 1933

at the age of 84

In the drawing of the tombstone provided by Elise Crosnier, only the French inscription is visible, which may again underscore the argument that Aurelie Picard died a French Catholic Christian.[3]

PART TWO: ISABELLE EBERHARDT

Chapter 7

ISABELLE EBERHARDT (1877-1901)
AND THE LURE OF ALGERIA

The account presented here is not intended to be an in-depth biography of Isabelle Eberhardt, a task already well performed by Cecily Mackworth in The Destiny of Isabelle Eberhardt (1950, 2nd. Ed. 1977). We attempt here rather to highlight the differences between Isabelle Eberhardt and Aurélie Picard. These were of major proportions, but they still serve to place Eberhardt just as firmly and indissolubly in the colonial context as was Picard. Nonetheless, a compressed formal biography is necessary in order to provide a framework for the contrast.

When Isabelle Eberhardt was born in Geneva on 17 February 1877, Aurélie Picard Tijani was twenty-nine, had been a married woman for almost nine years, and was already influential in her corner of South-Central Algeria. On that particular day, she was quite unaware of the appearance of a new star destined also to shine in Colonial Algeria, though in a strikingly different way.

Unlike the threadbare and conventional lower middle-class background of Aurélie Picard, that of Isabelle Eberhardt was upper-class and polyglot. Isabelle was illegitimate, as was her mother Nathalie, a half-Jewish German woman. Nathalie Eberhardt married a Tsarist Russian General, Paul de Moerder, having failed to tell him of her illegitimacy or her Jewish ancestry until after the marriage. During this period of the 1860's there was tremendous anti-Semitism in the Tsarist army, and General de Moerder lived in terror of the discovery of his wife's origins. As it was, he was thoroughly disliked by senior and subordinate officers alike.

Members of the family also seem to have tended toward mental instability, as evidenced by the suicides of Isabelle's half brothers Vladimir and Augustin, in 1897 and 1914, respectively, and of her niece in 1924.[1]

73

General de Moerder was a wealthy man, and he employed a tutor for his three children, Nikolas, Nathalie, and Vladimir. This tutor, Alexander Trofimovsky, was a handsome and talented man, a former priest in the Russian Orthodox Church who spoke seven languages (Russian, French, Greek, Latin, German, Turkish, and Arabic). He had rejected Christianity and adopted a nihilism with socialist overtones--a doctrine which was rapidly gaining supporters in Russian intellectual circles. He was a dynamic man with controversial ideas, and he was younger than the general.

The inevitable happened. Trofimovsky abandoned his wife and four children, eloping with Nathalie who brought along her own three children. They escaped to Turkey and then moved to Italy. Although Nathalie's lover might have had a scintillating and unconventional mind, she was unprepared for the ostracism they received in Italian society after the social life she had led as a high-ranking Russian officer's wife; life became intolerable in such a Catholic country and they moved on, finally reaching Switzerland where they settled.

General de Moerder still loved his errant wife and had kept track of her. He went to Switzerland to make an effort at reconciliation, but though another son was born (Augustin), matters did not mend. He was concerned about his wife's uncertain financial position and when he died he left her a considerable fortune. Even though the capital was tied up in Russia, a comfortable income arrived regularly thereafter with provisions made for his four children when they became adults.

Nathalie and her lover spent a further five years wandering before settling in Geneva for good. There Isabelle was born, and she was given her mother's maiden name of Eberhardt, even though Trofimovsky was her father. With such a large family in tow, their European nomadism, with its concomitant obligation of sheltering a small tribe, became impossible. Therefore, Alex, or Vava as the family called him, bought a large and rambling house hidden in a big, overgrown jungle of a garden. As he had little or no money, this was no doubt paid for out of de Moerder's funds, perhaps justifiably so, as only Isabelle was biologically Vava's. The neighbors naturally disapproved of the couple living together unmarried, and with children too. This fact hurt Isabelle's mother, who, as she got older, bored her children by her constant talk of the gay life she had led among the elite. Although

Trofimovsky disapproved of formal education, the children all spoke and wrote seven languages fluently. Their stepfather also had theories on developing the land they lived on, and he put all the family to work; these ideas were doomed to failure as no one had any idea about agriculture nor any interest in the subject. They were much more given to day-dreaming, immature philosophizing, and the pursuit of books. The children rarely left the house, a fact they did not seem to find unusual; but then they may have been afraid to put up a fight in order to do so, as Vava had become a moody and irascible man whom they disliked.

The children's choppy, inconsistent lives led to inconsistent characters. Perhaps a certain weakness and instability had been handed down through the de Moerder family. However, their stepfather abhorred any sign of weakness and berated them to the point that they thought they were useless. The eldest daughter was the first to escape in marriage. The house was always alive with rows, but the row her elopement caused transcended everything that had gone before. Her name was never mentioned again in front of him.

Isabelle was only eleven when this happened and was not much concerned. She showed none of her brothers' weakness of character, a fact Trofimovsky was quick to note. Here, he believed, was someone of his blood whom he could mold according to his ideas. Isabelle had no wish to be delicate and feminine herself, and Vava saw no reason why she should be treated any differently from a boy. Isabelle became a tomboy, wore her hair cut short, and dressed in boys' clothes. She was only eleven, but she was the only one to do the work of a young man around the grounds. From her father she learnt history, geography, and philosophy, and she showed great ability for drawing and painting. She read everything she could lay her hands on. Although French was the main language in the household, Isabelle read Greek or Russian with equal enjoyment. She stayed up half the night conducting lengthy political and philosophical discussions with young Russian students, but, even so, she felt that the students were as boring, if not as conventional, as the natives of Geneva.

Isabelle's adolescence was not happy; she loved her mother and her brother Augustin, and her father's contemptuous attitude toward them saddened her, especially his contempt for Augustin who was everything he despised: shy, inarticulate, nervous, and weak. Isabelle also seems to have felt stifled and, at the age of thirteen, to have wanted to leave home. It was at this time that a notice in a French paper caught her eye:

> Young French officer stationed in the Algerian Sahara, bored to death, seeks correspondent.[2]

The young man's name was Eugène Letord, a lieutenant attached to one of the Bureaux Arabes south of Constantine. The news seemed to her a godsend, as a means of escape from what she considered a drab life in a despotic home. The East, the desert, was opening up before her eyes; she plunged wholeheartedly into a wild correspondence about her fantasies and her family. Each week the letters were different, vivid and ardent. She spouted philosophy, quoted Pierre Loti by the page, and commented irreverently on life in Geneva. For some reason, she signed herself "Nadia." The proper young Letord was both shocked and intrigued by Isabelle's unorthodox ideas and found her letters far more interesting than any he could have received from a bourgeois French girl with whom he would have exchanged dull and reticent platitudes. Isabelle was avid for every detail of his life, and he was an observant young man, more interested in the life and customs of the Algerian Muslims around him than his superior officers thought necessary. He knew he was unpopular and considered eccentric by the garrison, so his hard exile in the cruel heat was made lighter by his correspondence with "Nadia." To Isabelle he could explain his misgivings over arrogant methods of colonization which evidently distressed him because they denied the Algerians equal rights with the French colonizers. He and Isabelle spoke the same language: to both of them an Algerian was a Muslim, and not, as to the French settler, an "Arab" in the colonial vernacular.

Eugène urged her and her sad, drifting brother to move to Algiers or Bone where he had friends. She kept secret from her father what had become more than just a vague idea and pleased him by working hard with him at Arabic.

Isabelle's Saharan correspondence opened up a new line of thought, because amid the circle of Russian students was a young Turk attached to the consulate in Geneva. He loved poetry and was a dreamer; his name was Rashid Bey, but for some reason, possibly making a play on his name, Isabelle called him Archivar. Living alone in a country of infidels, he nevertheless remained a devout Muslim. Nothing delighted him more than to instruct Isabelle in the basic tenets of Islam, and he combined this with philosophy and poetry. Isabelle was ripe to fall into the arms of this sensational man, as she was madly in love, although probably more with Islam than with Archivar. He did not take this seventeen-year-old girl's passion too seriously.

To her brother Augustin, Isabelle poured out her heart, her longing for the desert, the dust and the sun, and above all the exotic fascination that the lands of Islam held for her. She wanted to go there disguised as a man. Her personal relationships with her family, and in particular with Augustin for whom she had a strong and almost unnatural love, were impetuous and full of ups and downs. They do not concern us here, though they influenced her personal life and later writings, some of which are to be found among the French overseas archives at Aix-en-Provence. She wrote passionate, turbulent and furious letters to Augustin who had joined the Foreign Legion (if only to prove himself to her stepfather) and had thus reached Algeria and the beloved desert before Isabelle.

Meanwhile, the situation at Villa Neuve was deteriorating; Alex Trofimovsky had become a raging tyrant terrorizing the entire family and poor Mme de Moerder became more and more depressed by the strain. Early that spring the unhappy Vladimir committed suicide by closing the smoke vent in the stove in his room. Evil mouths whispered that his father had driven him to it.[3] This was enough for Isabelle; gloom and melancholy invaded the already embittered house, so it was no hard task to persuade Isabelle's constantly weeping and nervously exhausted mother that it was time to make their escape and let Vava manage for himself. Through mutual friends of Augustin, Isabelle already had an address in Algeria where they could go. They furtively made their preparations for departure, while Trofimovsky, wrapped in his own dejected thoughts, scarcely noticed.

Leaving disaster and tragedy behind, Isabelle and her mother started their journey toward North Africa and the sun. She and her mother arrived in Bone (called 'Annaba, since Algerian Independence in 1962) in the spring of 1897 (at the same time that Sidi Ahmad al-Tijani was at death's door). One look at the neat little houses of the civil servants of that already very French town and Isabelle searched out a simple house in the <u>qasba</u> for her self and her mother. (How horrified Aurélie would have been at this break with tradition and 'mixing with the natives'!)

This was paradise to Isabelle; the busy little street, the vendors calling out their wares, the neighborhood <u>suq</u> (market) and her small mud house filled her heart with peace and joy. Five times a day she listened to the profession of faith introducing the call to prayer: "<u>Allahu Akbar: Ashadu anna la ilaha illa 'Allah wa Muhammad ar-rasulu 'llah!</u>" ("God is Great: I testify that there is no God but God, and that Muhammad is the Messenger of God!") Or, particularly with respect to the dawn prayer call: "Come to prayer! Come to salvation! Prayer is better than sleep!"

Totally unlike Aurélie Picard Tijani, Isabelle Eberhardt embraced Islam with complete sincerity that was so intense she inspired her gentle mother as well. Her mother studied Arabic, and they both took religious instruction until they became proficient in that faith. Then one day they both pronounced the profession of faith exactly as given in the preceding paragraph. Both technically and in the terms of her inner convictions, Isabelle was now at one with Islam, and in that religion she found continual consolation. It should be remembered that Aurélie Picard was undeniably Christian and French. She repudiated Islamic custom and harshly tried to impose her own ways on the Algerian Muslims around her.

Isabelle Eberhardt evidently genuinely wanted to throw off, for good and all, her Western way of life, feeling deep down that she belonged to Islamic culture. Such identification could not have come from her German mother and grandmother, but possibly from her Russian father, a nomad and an incurable romantic and a dreamer.

Again contrary to Aurélie, Isabelle immediately adopted Arab dress, and the comfortable loose robes of Algerian men enabled her with her slight, slim figure, to carry off the disguise well. In this garb she was free to wander the streets and <u>suqs</u> at will. The Europeans were of course scandalized, but Isabelle was indifferent to their opinions --it was the opinions of the Algerians that concerned her, and they would have been equally scandalized had she wandered around the <u>qasba</u> alleys unescorted, either openly as a European woman, or even more so, as a Muslim woman.

Isabelle's pen friend, Eugène Letord, opened many doors in Bone for her through letters of introduction. She applied what classical Arabic she had already studied to colloquial Algerian, and this gradually enabled her to converse freely and easily with local scholars, who were impressed at her knowledge of Islam and her evidently sincere intentions to follow that faith as devoutly as possible. She soon had offers of marriage from rich young Muslims, but Isabelle was not yet tying herself down to the life of a Muslim woman, however powerful she might become behind the scenes. Like Aurélie, though for very different reasons, she was very much to the fore. She wanted her freedom and she wanted to roam, as she had ambitions to become a writer. She jotted down on any piece of paper or notebook that came to her hand her numerous observations of the life she saw around her. One of her earliest stories was "Yasmina." In this story, she may have had Eugène, the misfit, in mind since it is a love story between a French officer and a Bedouin girl.

Isabelle and her mother had not even been a year in Algeria when the latter died of a heart attack in November, 1897, and was buried in the Muslim cemetery overlooking the harbor. Isabelle's grief was intense, and she never really got over her mother's death. Now there was nothing to hold her to the little house in the qasba, and with the utter abandon with which she did everything, she threw herself into a nomadic life.

Isabelle's wanderings may have taken her into Tunisia and certainly close to its borders. There was no doubt that Europeans and Arabs alike (each in their own way) talked of her scandalous behavior. Some of this flow of gossip may have reached the ears of Aurélie Picard Tijani; and Isabelle in turn must have heard of Mme Tijani, for what other European woman lived isolated in the desert? Wherever she went, Isabelle lived in the qasba, making out that she was the daughter of a Russian Muslim, though the local rumor-mill made her out to be of Jewish origin.

To Isabelle, Islam was first of all exotic, even mystical, and she approached it with the genuinely mystic fervor of a member of the Sufi order. In so doing, however, she never failed in the rigorous external observation of visible symbols that Islam demands: she observed the fast of Ramadan, prayed scrupulously five times a day and was generally very devout. But she was indifferent to the Prophet's injunction against alcoholic beverages. She lived and dressed as a man and placed no restraint on her personal behavior. Isabelle wore the classic Algerian head-dress of a tarbush swathed in yards of white muslin held in place by silk or woolen cords. Her Arab shirt and baggy trousers were cloaked in a long burnous. She spent hours in small, dark Arab cafes sitting or lolling on the matting, an elbow comfortably propped on a cushion. Along with the harsh local black tobacco that Eberhardt was never without, she became quickly addicted to <u>kif</u> and the deliciously acrid, pungent perfume that rose from the pipes of the other smokers.

People who knew her observed that she had a raucous, nasal voice which was so surprising and inconsistent with her large, soft, and lustrous black eyes. In this harsh voice she talked long and learnedly to pious elders, or let younger men make love to her as the fancy took her. Time proved that Eberhardt and Picard had one other thing in common: they were both barren. Despite Aurélie's two marriages to husbands who had families by other wives and Isabelle's promiscuous behavior and one marriage, neither bore any children. The both loved Algeria, for different reasons, but Isabelle wandered in the slum quarters of the very poor, and in any hovel she would scribble madly until the candles burnt out. Was she an agent provocateur, sent by the British or the Germans, perhaps, to stir up anti-French feelings? No one could make her out, as she never told the same story twice about herself; she no doubt derived considerable amusement from the fact that the Europeans, so bent on tagging their own kind with labels, were unable to place her. The Arabs, though equally mystified, were more tolerant: her soul was troubled, Allah would care for her, and it was not for them as Muslims to criticize. The French administration was definitely disturbed by Eberhardt. Her professions of Islam gave her an entrée into circles where, in their opinion, she could do very great harm. This is very possibly true, but she was essentially apolitical. In her heart she was opposed to the steady French penetration, their usurpation of Muslim land, and their relentless imposition of their own laws. She felt that the famous French <u>Mission Civilisatrice</u>, was more insidious than even the White Man's Burden of British colonialism in India, where, for the most part the peoples' lands were not usurped and exploited, or at least not in the same way. In her part of the desert, the colonization of Algeria was in its very early stages with the French still struggling for a firm grip. Isabelle Eberhardt hated the smugness and arrogance of the land-grabbers and would surely have been a staunch supporter of the nationalism and independence that was to come fifty years later.

The settlers were anathema to Isabelle, who was almost certainly on the French blacklist because she refused to work with the French authorities. Her every movement was watched by agents in French pay, just waiting for her to put a foot wrong; but one could hardly deport a woman because she had "gone native," embraced Islam, and dressed like a man. Furthermore Isabelle, in a sense, lived two lives. On the one hand, her ambition was to write and be a writer, acclaimed by the world; yet her real self was the contemplative dreamer who loved solitude. In those moods, she wanted only to be alone, to be able to think, and in the low haunts of the medina she was able to achieve this. In so doing, Isabelle acquired for herself a reputation for debauchery and drunkenness, a reputation that stuck to her all her life despite her generosity. But she did not care. Why should she? She was living her life, though she was letting down the European image.

What the religious Isabelle did not realize, however, was that she was also an embarrassment to her Muslim co-religionists, especially the more traditional ones. Yet they too were helpless because she was a foreigner. The small amount of money left to her by her mother was running out and fate, qisma or al-maktub (that which is written), seemed intent on forcing her back to Geneva.

Early in 1899, Isabelle did return to Geneva where she and Augustin met again. She also met there the man she had fallen for passionately in her adolescence, Rashid Bey, or Archivar. She had changed astonishingly in less than three years, and now they were Muslims together, each with a phi-losophy that owed little to the Qur'an. He found her fascinating and formally asked for her hand. Trofimovsky, who had aged terribly, consented, but Isabelle valued freedom more than marriage and refused.[4]

Isabelle was particularly disgusted with her brother's disenchantment with Algeria and his desire to settle down in France. The house was a ruin, and Trofimovsky a sick and sad man haunted by the past. He died during this period, and the consequent legal problems that arose over Villa Neuve were too much

for Isabelle's taut nerves. This and her disillu-
sionment over Augustin drove her back to North
Africa to seek refuge even further in the desert.
She now assumed the identity of a Tunisian student,
Si Mahmud al-Sa'di, and she used the masculine
gender when referring to herself. It is curious how
she never mentioned in her notes and diaries the
Muslim names she and her mother assumed when they
converted to Islam.

Si (Mr.) Mahmud al-Sa'di-cum-Isabelle traveled
to Biskra, which was even then a major French-
sponsored tourist resort (although today, slightly
over eighty years later, it is anything but a
resort), a green jewel in the middle of a gravelly
desert. She stayed a while and then pushed on to El
Oued much further south. Although the latter is an
oasis and still a delight to the eye, it was a blast
furnace and a hardship post for the military.
Eugène Letord was stationed there and Isabelle aimed
to meet her girlhood pen pal. He promised all the
help he could give her. His strange correspondence
with this unknown woman made him intensely curious
about her; she was so different from the gentle and
demure young ladies of the Second Empire era whom he
had known in France.

As Isabelle was to discover, the road to El
Oued was not easy. The Saharan Territories to the
south were still under military administration, and
permission was required from the Bureau Arabe. The
French military authorities were suspicious of
Isabelle's request to travel into the Sahara during
the summer, when the climate was almost unbearable.
Her disguise as a male Arab made them even more so.
It was even suspected that she might be a missionary
masquerading as an Arab, for foreign missionaries
had caused trouble before through trying, in vain of
course, to gain converts to Christianity. They were
suspected as well of subversive political activities
in favor of their own countries. Isabelle indi-
gnantly refuted the accusation, saying proudly that
she was a Muslim and a Russian, which had the
authorities completely baffled. To ease the situation Captain Susbeille, who had been present at the
interview, offered Isabelle a place in his convoy
that was leaving for Tuggurt the following day.
Isabelle accepted, though probably not very
graciously, as she wanted a far more adventurous
mode of travel.

The rest of the evening she spent in wandering
around the Jewish quarter where unveiled women were
dressed in colorful clothes, with fringed shawls and

caps and scarves glittering with silver and gold embroidery. People had emerged from their houses and hovels into the relative cool of the veningair, and Isabelle's stroll eventually took her to the medina and the cafés. In one, she made the acquaintance of two Arabs with whom she chatted for a long time telling them of her plans the following morning of joining Captain Susbeille's convoy. At once she sensed a chill in the conversation, although with some persistence she finally got out of them the fact that Susbeille was thoroughly disliked by the local people and considered an arch-colonialist who believed that the only way to deal with a "native" successfully was to crush him. It simply was not done to be polite or considerate. Susbeille was precisely the type that Isabelle held in contempt, the type she later wrote about so derisively. In the morning she made some vague excuse about having found a more congenial means of travel. This was a rash and tactless move which would go against her later, as the captain brooded over her snub and bided his time until he could take revenge.

Eberhardt had no particular deadline for reaching her destination, which was really anywhere provided it was away from civilization and in the desert. She spent the heat of the day happily loitering in the cafés with her new-found friends and some spahis as well as the son of a local marabout (saint), and then when it was cool, at about two o'clock in the morning, they set off on the long desert journey. The group may not have had the snap and smartness of a French convoy, but it was just as safe, if not safer, since no desert traveler goes forth haphazardly. The desert does not forgive anyone who skimps on water to make a lighter load. The pace was leisurely, as it was pointless to be in a hurry.

This was the kind of freedom that Isabelle had dreamed of--space and the horizon far, far away. She had a tough little Arab Barb horse that would gallop across the firm, silvery sand. She took shelter anywhere, close to her horse when travelling, for the desert nights were cold, even in mid-summer. With her habitual inattention to personal health, Isabelle eventually contracted a fever that often left her weak and ill, though her joy in life remained untarnished.

As she parted from one lot of traveling companions, she picked up with others; sometimes with soldiers of the Foreign Legion on patrol, sometimes with Bedouin tribesmen. She was intoxicated with her freedom, and above all, with the fact that no one suspected her of being a hated Christian foreigner. She was just Si Mahmud, and it was not unusual for traditionally educated young Muslim men to travel long distances to the zawiyas of saints of religious orders to pray, study, improve their learning of the Qur'an, and gain further insights into the teachings of their order under the guidance of an 'alim, a religious teacher.

The area between Biskra and Tuggurt is rich shurfa country, and Isabelle may well have stayed a day or two at the house of a member of the Tijaniya, where she possibly heard about Aurélie. Aurélie Tijani was never mentioned in any of Isabelle's writings, though in Tuggurt she was close to Tamasin and Tamalhat, Tijani territory and hence solidly under French domination.

So Eberhardt remained disguised as an Arab, though "disguised" in French eyes only, since Isabelle considered her style of masculine dress her normal apparel; she was a Muslim and it was prudent and practical to travel in such clothes. Often she stayed in the company of members of the Qadiriya Order, whose anti-French leanings had not diminished since the surrender of 'Abd al-Qadir in 1847. Furthermore, Isabelle came face to face with Captain Susbeille again in Tuggurt. He was in charge of the Bureau Arabe there, and their meeting was full of hate and anger. He refused permission for one of the shaikhs of the Sha'anba tribe to guide her to Ouargla (Wargla). Isabelle controlled her anger with icy politeness, and, with the greatest of difficulty, at least obtained a guide to take her directly through the Suf and the oasis of El Oued, the site of dozens of mosques and considerable Islamic learning . . . and close to which were Gaymar and Tamalhat, as already noted.

A great disappointment awaited Isabelle on her arrival. She discovered that Eugène Letord had been transferred elsewhere. Despite the recommendations he left behind on her behalf, she was not welcomed. In fact Captain Cauvet, commander of the El Oued garrison, was astounded to hear that a young woman wanted to see him. He was even more astonished, in fact scandalized, to find that the young Arab who stood before him was Isabelle, the woman in question! Though he found her company entertaining and intriguing, he still considered her presence most undesirable, and a responsibility he wanted no part in, especially as Isabelle was still sick with acute fever.

Though her vision was blurred by this fever, the Suf appealed to her artistic temperament. The fiery wind, the dust and the sky colorless with heat and haze enraptured her. Henceforth she would be a nomad of this region; no matter what her troubles and setbacks, it would be back to the Suf that she would go. She wrote after her first visit to El Oued that the first sight of El Oued was for her the complete and final revelation, the harsh and splendid Suf with its strange beauty combined with immense sadness.

She was happiest among the Sha'anba and their camels, and with the disdain that she shared with them of European futility.

Almost prostrate with fever, she traveled to the Aures, where in the healthy mountain air she recovered somewhat. Finally she paid a brief visit to the little cemetery in Bone and then, at long last, she met Eugène Letord. They discovered they were indeed kindred spirits--for her he was the first European to whom she could talk without being thought completely mad.

Isabelle was almost penniless, as affairs at the Villa Neuve had made no progress; there was no money in sight, and her brother had married. She received a letter begging her to go to France to meet her sister-in-law. She scraped up the money to travel deck passage to Marseille, feeling that her brother had betrayed her with the marriage and already resenting his wife.

Her spirits dropped even further when she found that they lived in a poor and depressing quarter of the city and that her sister-in-law was nothing more than a petite bourgeois concerned with respectability and a "What Will the Neighbors Think" mentality. Isabelle was dumbfounded and jealous that her Augustin had chosen a working-class girl without ambitions--it riled her to see her brother happy with such an insipid girl.

"Jenny" as Isabelle insisted on calling her, was just as horrified by Isabelle, her cropped hair, outrageous clothes, and a cigarette. Isabelle, for her part, behaved badly. She delighted in looking like an urchin and shocking her sister-in-law and the neighbors. It was not a happy reunion; they had frequent rows of a magnitude that "Jenny" had never experienced, followed by impassioned upbraidings and jealous tears till Augustin could stand it no longer and begged his sister to leave them in peace and to their own way of life.

Furious and unhappy, Isabelle stormed off to Geneva one cold winter day. Villa Neuve was a pillaged shambles, and the garden more of a ruin than ever. She found herself unable to pick up threads in her Russian and mildly revolutionary circles of yore and dejectedly took herself off to Paris, in hopes of finding a publisher for her writings.

There she had the good fortune to meet the widow of Antoine de Villambrosa, Marquis de Morès. The marquis, while on an expedition in southern Tunisia and Algeria in 1896, had been murdered near the frontier. Mme de Morès was astonished to find that Isabelle knew the villages through which the marquis had traveled. On learning that Isabelle ardently desired to return to the desert and also that she had had no financial success with Parisian publishers, the marquise offered to finance an expedition for Isabelle to solve the four-year-old mystery of her husband's death.

As it was, Isabelle did not leave immediately; there was an interval again in Geneva before she could make up her mind to go back to Algeria, during which she spent most of Mme de Morès' money. She was counting on a legacy from her father. Augustin, upset by Isabelle's stormy visit, had taken himself off to Sardinia leaving her to cope with the muddle of Villa Neuve. She discovered that the elusive lawyer, Samuel (who had never replied to any of their letters), had dissipated whatever money there was, so there was nothing for it but to cut her losses and go. Her departure grieved her more than she thought possible because she was breaking her last tangible links with her family and friends.

Chapter 8

ATTEMPTED ELIMINATION AND EXPULSION FROM ALGERIA

Isabelle wasted no time in Algiers but headed as fast as possible to Tuggurt where, to her surprise, she had no difficulty in obtaining permission to go to El Oued. There she rented a house belonging to the local quid and dreamed her days away living on credit and the hope that the money from the sale of Villa Neuve would be forwarded to her by her faithful friend Eugène who had undertaken to send on any letters that might arrive. Nothing ever turned up because no money was forthcoming from the shady lawyer in the first place. The object of the journey south seemed to have faded from Isabelle's mind, but it was very much to the fore in the minds of the French military authorities, as rumors travel fast in North Africa ("le téléphone arabe"). They were highly displeased to learn that Eberhardt was being paid by Mme de Morès to investigate her husband's murder. As usual, she suffered the hostility of the colonials because she refused to conform. She saw them as arrogant, puffed up with conceit, and disdainful of the brotherhood of Islam from which they were totally excluded. She was amazed at their unbelievable insolence toward the Arabs and the complete unawareness of the scorn and barely concealed hatred in which they, in their turn, were held by all Algerian Muslims as well as by the desert people with whom Isabelle particularly identified. This in comparison with Aurélie who was quite impervious to the fact that she was an intruder, a European and, above all, an infidel.

One day money arrived from Eugène, who must have guessed her plight from the lack of correspondence for her. Of course nothing arrived from the proceeds of the sale of Villa Neuve. With this money she paid her debts and bought herself a horse to replace the hard-mouthed one she had been lent by the qaid. She named him "Suf" after the region of the desert she so loved, and they became inseparable companions. With him she explored the desert and

87

became an intrepid rider. Indeed, she gained the admiration of the French and the wholehearted sympathy of the Arabs.

It was on one of her lonely rides that she met her husband-to-be. Late one evening she rode down a canyon into a fertile grove of palm trees and cultivated plots of land surrounding a well. She watered the horse, drank the relatively cool water, and let the skin bag drip over her. Then she rolled herself in her burnous and lay down by the well to sleep. She had been asleep a few hours when a sound disturbed her and she woke to see a tall and slim spahi leaning over her. She was not afraid, and in the bright starlight she could see that he had a fine mustache and soft brown eyes. She sat up and greeted him and he politely returned her salutation and sat down beside her. His name was Sliman Ahanni and he was a quartermaster-sergeant in the spahis. Though they talked in Arabic to begin with, it transpired he spoke good French and had a certain amount of education. It was an instant, magnetic attraction, and the affair that developed was quite different from any other that Isabelle had experienced. He was gentle and kind, and Isabelle was thirsty for those qualities; Sliman spoke of eternal love but she had been disillusioned too often to take their romance too seriously. It was the present that counted--tomorrow could take care of itself.

Sliman's regimental duties kept him busy during the day, but they spent romantic nights riding across the desert and making love in other cool, desert gardens similar to the one in which they had met. Naturally their liaison became public knowledge when Sliman began to visit Isabelle in the rented house. Once again she was the focal point of gossip, scandal and hostility, and probably even jealousy. For although Isabelle had no claim to beauty--except for her lustrously dark eyes--or any special feminine charms, those Frenchmen who had sought her favor were sorely piqued at seeing a half-educated Algerian preferred to themselves.

On account of the de Morès affair and Isabelle's involvement with it, her every movement had been watched by informers who reported back to Captain Cauvet, the commander of the El Oued garrison. But even he came to realize that Isabelle's sorties into the desert, sometimes for days on end, were not to incite the tribesmen but for her own pleasure and the pleasure she took in the company of an Arab. Her love affair with Sliman kept the garrison gossip-pot boiling. Word got to Mme de Morès, probably through the Bureau Arabe, that Isabelle had lost interest in the mission she had set out on, and her source of income was withdrawn. However, Sliman Ahanni had his meager pay and somehow they managed--Isabelle mostly in a dream of _kif_. Sliman himself seems to have been a sickly man with a rather colorless personality which was, perhaps, for the best as Isabelle pushed him to read and improve his education. Like Aurélie, she wore the pants.

Isabelle Eberhardt's connections with the Qadiriya order evidently dated from the time of her arrival in El Oued, in which region it was very well established. She visited Sidi Husain bin Brahim, the muqaddam of the Qadiriya order at Gaymar (where there was also an important Tijaniya lodge). Apparently she convinced him both of the genuineness of her adherence to Islam and of her inclinations toward Islamic mysticism as the path to that ultimate unity with God through evanescence (_fana'_) of the individual. As Mackworth has correctly noted, there was nothing unusual about Isabelle becoming a female _faqira_, a female member of the Qadiriya.[1] Although membership in orders, as with most overt religious activity including mosque attendance, prayer, visits to shrines and the pilgrimage to Mecca is predominantly and visibly a male concern in Islam, this fact by no means disqualifies women from participation: the emphasis is on sex segregation and by no means on exclusion. Muslim women are just as devout as men; the locus, rather than the focus, of their devotion is simply more restricted.

However, Sidi Husain, while aware that his student was a woman and a European, was so impressed with her sincerity and knowledge of the Qur'an that he accepted her as Si Mahmud, and she went through the initiation as a faqir, a male member of the order. Her head was shaved by the muqaddam who then heard her recite an act of contrition and the Qadiriya vow. After this she was given the _tasbih_ or rosary of the order and was instructed in its _dhikr_, or litany, and supererogatory prayer which all _ikhwan_ or "brothers" must recite after each of the five daily prayers. Although the formal organization of all Muslim religious orders is more or less the same, with the top shaikh at the main or parent _zawiya_, and the muqaddamin acting as his representatives at offshoot _zawiyas_, the rosaries and the litany of each are at some variance, even if only slight, from all the others.

In the Qadiriya case, the dhikr consists of the simple though time-consuming practice of repeating the tawhid, the phrase "La ilaha illa 'llah," ("There is no God but God"), 165 times following every prayer.[2]

At any rate, Isabelle Eberhardt recited the prayer of engagement and received the tasbih of the Qadiriya order at El Oued. Even though the Amir 'Abd a-Qadir had been its most outspoken Algerian exponent, and, because of his adherence to it the order was viewed as anti-French, in 1900 when Eberhardt joined, it was apolitical in tone. Given the complete negation, by that time, of the Algerian Muslim personality and culture under a triumphant France Outre-Mer it could hardly have been otherwise. Even so, the Qadiriya were neither blatantly pro-French nor had they any reformist tendencies, as the Tijaniya were and had. (A brief summary on the Qadiriya order is given in Appendix C.) This seems to be shown by a singularly nasty episode in which Isabelle Eberhardt only narrowly escaped death.

Sidi Husain bin Brahim believed Isabelle's story of having had a Russian Muslim father and, in a fatherly way, he took her under his wing. Through him (and probably to his regret) she was now to meet his brother, Sidi a'-Hashimi bin Brahim, whose physical presence and spellbinding rhetoric had already convinced many of the ikhwan that he should be regarded as top shaikh of the order at El Oued even though his own brothers and a considerable local faction were convinced otherwise: that his piety was only skin-deep, that his double dealings were legion, and that he was purely out for himself. Isabelle, however, tone-deaf as always so far as personalities were concerned, perceived none of this, a fact which may well have contributed to the attempt on her life which was made in Bahima east of El Oued. For the time being she was captivated by the imposing figure of Sidi al-Hashimi upon his horse leading a galloping exhibition of powder play, as well as by the procession and the hadra (ritual dance) of the Qadiriya.[3]

A third Qadiriya brother, Sidi al-Iman bin Brahim, wanted to make a pilgrimage to Nafta, just over the Tunisian border, where his father was buried, and both Isabelle and Sidi al-Hashimi wished to join him.

Here Isabelle intended to present her request for admittance to the Qadiriya order to Sidi al-Iman and return if possible the same day to spend as much time as she could with Sliman before he went to Batna. Sliman was a very sick man, probably with malaria which was rampant there, and he may have appeared weak and ineffectual to others. Isabelle, however, saw him as her dream man, and with him she found love, romance, and an anchor in that vast desert land.

Isabelle rode to Bahima on 27 January 1901, with Sidi al-Hashimi, and it was there that she was suddenly plucked from obscurity to become the main actor in a murder case which became famous throughout Algeria and which she herself reported in detail in a dispatch from Marseille to the Dépêche Algérienne on June 4. She and Sidi al-Hashimi had entered the house of a certain Si Brahim bin l-'Arbi, and while their host retired for the afternoon prayer, Isabelle was seated in an antechamber with five or six members of the Rahmaniya order who were on friendly terms with the Qadiriya. One of these men asked her to translate some commercial telegrams so her head was lowered as she read them. Hence she failed to see the stranger, dressed in rags, who ran up and slashed her on the crown of her head with his sword. As luck would have it, she was saved from death by a clothes line strung across the room which partially intercepted the blow. Stunned, she tried unsuccessfully to grab Sidi al-Hashimi's sabre from the opposite wall while the would-be assassin, though disarmed by a young muqaddam of the Qadiriya and one of Sidi al-Hashimi's servants, nonetheless made good his escape. However, he was recognized by several individuals as a member of the Tijaniya, who, as we know, were not on good terms with the Qadiriya, and Si Brahim bin l-'Arbi sent for the young secular shaikh of Bahima--who was also a Tijani--demanding that the man be denounced to the Bureau Arabe. Against his will, the shaikh gave in and the would-be murderer, a local man named 'Abdallah bin Muhammad, was brought in. At first he pleaded insanity, but seeing that this would not work, switched his plea to one of an ordainment from God to kill Si Mahmud/Isabelle Eberhardt. This he stuck to, even though, as he was to say at his trial, he did not know her and had nothing against her, especially as he knew she was a Muslim.

From her hospital bed, Isabelle completely forgave her assailant. Although the sword blow which was meant to cleave her head in two instead almost severed her left arm, Isabelle regarded the unfortunate 'Abdallah bin Muhammad as a shahid, a voluntary martyr, sent by God to open a road for her at the price of his own suffering.

About this time she began to see herself as a
mrabta, a female saint, or even as one of the abdal,
the secret or "substitute" saints who insure within
Islam constant liaison between heaven and earth, and
Mackworth regards the attempted assassination as the
point when Eberhardt conceived this view of her
destiny.[4] But it is also interesting to note, as
Mackworth does, a dissenting and much more mundane
view of Eberhardt's attempted murder: that expressed
to her years later by Captain Cauvet, the then
Bureau Arabe officer at El Oued, and supported by
the bashagha (native Algerian headman under French
supervision) of El Oued. Cauvet thought that the
attack on Isabelle had been instigated by Sidi al-
Hashimi himself in an attempt to compromise the
Tijaniya, who were of course under full French
protection and as a result were getting emoluments
that he wanted for himself. This interpretation was
seconded by the bashagha, who added that Sidi al-
Hashimi knew that Si Mahmud, or Isabelle, had come
to El Oued to discover the killers of the Marquis de
Morès and that he inferred that she had had French
support. Through her, he hoped to convince the
Bureau Arabe that the murderer was a Tijani who was
protected in blanket fashion by the whole of that
order. However, Sidi al-Hashimi soon came to
realize that Si Mahmud had no influence with the
French, who on the contrary, had done everything
possible to keep her out of the de Morès affair. It
was at this point continued the bashagha, that Sidi
al-Hashimi wanted to rid himself of Isabelle, all
the more so because she had become his mistress and
was an additional embarrassment in this capacity.
This latter point is unverifiable today.

Mackworth's bashagha informant also added,
most interestingly of all, that 'Abdallah bin
Muhammad was not a Tijani at all but a Qadiri,
acting on Sidi al-Hashimi's orders. We have unfortunately not been able to find archival corrobo-
ration of the above interpretation, but it seems
eminently believable and would certainly seem to fit
the facts of the case.[5]

Once Isabelle was strong enough after a slow
and painful recovery in the French hospital, she
lost no time in setting out for Batna where Sliman
had been stationed. Dr. Adolphe Teste, who had been
looking after her while she recuperated from her
wounds and who had become a close friend and
confidant, accompanied her as far as Gaymar where
she joined up with a small convoy bound for Batna by

slow, devious routes. The doctor was against Isabelle's leaving the hospital, as he did not consider her fully recovered and there, at least, she could receive treatment for her ever-recurring fevers and build up her strength through good and regular meals. But Isabelle would have none of it: she was pining over Sliman. As it proved, the trek by convoy was too much for her in her low state of health, and from Biskra she finished the journey by train. Sliman was waiting for her, but it was a frustrating reunion since he was confined to a regiment which was quartered in a part of the town off limits to civilians. Their passionate and clandestine meetings took place at night by the ramparts of the town.

Batna was indescribably depressing and dreary: built in a European style for the convenience of the military, and surrounded by a treeless plain across which the wind howled unceasingly, freezing cold or scorching hot. The winter of 1901 was exceptionally cold and wet, and Isabelle only possessed the thin clothes of the south and shoes too worn to keep out the mud and wet. She was destitute and lived in a poverty and squalor scarcely matched even in the poorest section of the Arab quarter. As she noted in her diary: "March 28, Here is complete destitution . . . No tea, no money, no fire . . . Nothing!"[6]

After two months of freezing and starving, Isabelle received a warning from the French authorities that she was to be expelled from North Africa. She had become an embarrassment to them because she was so openly and ardently a Muslim and because she made no effort to hide her contempt for the colonials. There was no official explanation, no reason, just an "invitation" to leave the country immediately. As a Russian citizen she was helpless, and even her own consul refused to intervene. She was frantic at the thought of going back to France penniless and in despair at having to leave Sliman. He, with his rank of sergeant in the spahis had automatically acquired French nationality.[7] He immediately applied for authorization to marry Isabelle, but this was flatly refused by the colonel, the lame excuse being that non-commissioned officers of the spahis should not be encouraged to marry foreigners or, in fact, have anything to do with them! There was nothing Isabelle could do to defend herself. Aurélie Picard had had a powerful friend in Cardinal Lavigerie and Sidi Ahmad was the shaikh of an important order, whereas Isabelle had

93

no influential friends and was on the blacklist of both the French administration and the colonial settlers. With the help of Sliman and others among her Algerian friends she scraped enough cash to buy a fourth-class ticket to Marseille (why the French did not pay her deportation fare is unmentioned in the archives). The few miserable possessions she had were tied in a bundle and, sad of heart, she set sail from Bone on 9 May 1901.

Chapter 9

ISABELLE EBERHARDT: HER MARRIAGE AND DEATH (1901-1904)

Augustin, having been unable to find work in Sardinia, had gone back to Marseille. When Isabelle arrived there she found him almost as poverty-stricken as herself, living under miserable, squalid conditions and, for the most part, still out of work. She was forced to live with him and his wife since she had nowhere else to go. Her sister-in-law took this in very bad grace, especially as Isabelle was so often sick with long bouts of debilitating malaria. Somehow or other, via the grapevine, Isabelle learnt, to her chagrin, that she need not have left Algeria in quite such haste as no official order had been signed for her deportation, but now she had no money and no one from whom she could borrow the return fare.

Despite her weakened condition she was able to pick up odd jobs and so keep herself in cigarettes. She presented a bizarre appearance with her closely shaved head and baggy, male attire. Isabelle had not been in France long when she received notice that her presence was required at 'Abdallah bin Muhammad's trial on Constantine, set for June 18, both as star witness and as victim. Along with the notification, money arrived, supposedly from the authorities, for the cheapest return fare. As we know, Isabelle had long forgiven the man and was loath to testify against him.

Although the attack had been hushed up at the time it happened, it now got full publicity in the Algerian press. The Dépêche Algérienne gave the most objective report (23 June 1901), while other newspapers availed themselves of the opportunity to strike out against Isabelle as though she were the accused rather than the victim. The court was filled to capacity with the wives of officers and civilian officials, as well as General Laborie de Labattut and most of the Constantine garrison. Lieutenant Colonel Janin of artillery was the

95

president of the court.

Though Isabelle declared publicly and vehemently that she bore her assailant no grudge and forgave him completely, and while the counsel for defense spoke most eloquently for his client, the Government Commissioner, M. Martin, demanded the death penalty. The culprit had already condemned himself, for M. Martin recalled one of the heated declarations of the accused: "The French have set over us in this country a shaikh and a secretary of the administration who do nothing but plunder us. It is because of hatred for the French that I attacked Mme Eberhardt, a Frenchwoman."

The council retired to deliberate the sentence and returned with an affirmative verdict, mitigated, however, by attenuating circumstances. 'Abdallah bin Muhammad was sentenced to life imprisonment with hard labor, causing a stir in the court. Isabelle was filled with impotent rage at this unjust verdict; her pleas for forgiveness and indulgence fell on deaf ears. General Laborie de Labattut walked over to Isabelle and declared loud enough for all to hear: "You cannot say that French justice has not thoroughly avenged you!"[1]

Isabelle, who did not want avenging at all, was shocked by the severity of the sentence. She was further shattered when, at the end of the trial, she was handed the official mandate from the governor-general expelling her forever from all French possessions in North Africa. The warning had now become fact. Isabelle made a further declaration to the Dépêche Algérienne even though it would not alter 'Abdallah's plight, in order to justify herself in the eyes of the ignorant and assert that she was not in the service of any foreign power. Part of the declaration is as follows:

> I cannot understand for what reason this measure has been taken against me, as I am Russian and have a perfectly clear conscience. I have never taken part in or known of any anti-French action, either in the Sahara or in the Tell. On the contrary, I defend the late na'ib of Ouargla, Sidi Muhammad Tayyib, who died gloriously under the French flag, with all my force against accusations of certain Muslims, ignorant of the real Islam—that of the Qur'an and the Sunna—who accused the na'ib of having betrayed Islam by installing the

96

French at In-Salah. I have spoken at
all times and everywhere to the natives
in favor of France, which is my adopted
country. Then why should I be the
object of a measure which, while deeply
wounding to my feelings as a Russian,
causes me immense pain of another sort,
since it separates me from my fiance
who, as a non-commissioned officer in
the garrison at Batna, cannot follow me?
I could have understood if I had been
forbidden to visit the military territory, in order to save me from the
vengeance of 'Abdallah's tribe, but I
have no desire to return to the South.
I ask nothing but to be allowed to live
at Batna and marry the man who has been
the companion of my ill fortune and who
is my only moral support in this
world . . . That is all.[2]

Separation from Sliman was unbearable, but
materially Isabelle was feeling a little more secure
because she was writing and publishing articles for
French journals and newspapers, even though still
only for a pittance.

Aware of Sliman's weak character, she never
let up in her correspondence to him and his
commanding officer urging for an exchange army post
in France. Through sheer determination and the
active support of Colonel Rancogne, Sliman finally
got his transfer to the colonel's regiment in
France. Now there was no further impediment to
their marriage since Sliman with his rank of
sergeant was a French citizen on French soil.

The civil marriage took place in Marseille at
the Town Hall and then at the mosque according to
Muslim rites. Now, as a legally married woman, and
in accordance with French law, Isabelle automatically assumed French nationality and no longer
could she be excluded from North Africa or any other
French colony. For her wedding, Isabelle dressed
for the first time since her childhood as a woman
and bought or borrowed a black skirt, mauve blouse,
and black hat, and had covered her shaved head with
a jet black wig. The sight must have been
startling, both to the registrar and to Sliman
himself!

Sliman's time in the army was drawing to a
close and his health was worse as he now suffered
badly from bronchitis. The future looked grim with

no foreseeable job and a very meager pension. They were both heavy smokers and preferred to go without food rather than cigarettes. In the age-old, time-honored Muslim way, they fell back on the only solution that presented itself: to live with his parents in Bone. The parents, too, were poor, but could hardly refuse the shelter of their roof to a son and his bride. Isabelle, for her part, was firmly convinced that once on North African soil and in a Muslim milieu, she would find a solution to their problems; so it was with few regrets that at the beginning of 1902 she bade farewell to Augustin and sailed from Europe, this time for good.

French penetration into Southwestern Algeria near the ill-defined Moroccan border beyond 'Ain Sfra was cautious but determined. However the battle at Taghit on 17 August 1903 in which a French outpost was besieged by a <u>harka</u> (regiment) of four thousand men from different tribes, with a follow-up a few days later at al-Mungar, where a French convoy was attacked by raiders during an imprudent halt, leaving thirty-six killed and forty-seven wounded, caused a hue and cry to be raised not only by the French army, but by the "colonial party" lobby and the Algerian settlers for immediate and effective occupation of the area. Many of the raiders were transborder Moroccans including members of the bands of Au 'Amama from Figuig in Morocco, who had been raiding the French desultorily since as far back as 1880.[3]

Charles Jonnart, the new governor general of Algeria, reacted vociferously, particularly after his own army was attacked in the same region, and secured the appointment of General Louis Hubert Gonsalve Lyautey as commander of the subdivision of 'Ain Sfra. It is no exaggeration to say that, as we shall see, Isabelle Eberhardt's intellectual involvement with Lyautey was considerable as was his influence on her.

The name of Lyautey was already one to be reckoned with, well before he became the first resident-general of the French Protectorate in Morocco in 1912. He had already won himself a reputation in Tonkin and in Madagascar serving under General Joseph Gallieni, and he was an enthusiastic proponent of the latter's progressive and unorthodox ideas about colonial warfare. Although he had had no experience with Muslim people, he took Gallieni's view that pacification of "indigenous peoples" was not so much a matter of battle or campaign strategy as one of peaceful penetration culminating in a political control which would lead eventually to economic and social development. During the time the general was active he was to exploit these ideas to the fullest; even by the time of his arrival at 'Ain Sfra his grand but vague design of politico-administrative engineering was ready to meet its first North African proving ground.

In the short term, at least, Lyautey's tactics were successful, and they differed from those of his more cautious predecessors in two important respects: the first was to make military power so evident as to encourage hostile tribesmen to surrender without fighting, and the other, if the first failed, was to do battle with them on their own terms, bit by bit, through careful and thorough pacification of one block of territory before moving on to the next.

As it happened Isabelle was already in 'Ain Sfra on a roving correspondent's assignment from El Akhbar when Lyautey came to assume command; she was in the role of Si Mahmud al-Sa'di, evidently on very good terms with Algerian Muslim spahis and French Foreign Legionnaires (to whom she spoke German, for most of them were German), and the news of her presence in the town soon came to Lyautey's attention. He interviewed her, and right away it seemed that they were kindred spirits. One can only assume that their equally unorthodox views on the reasons for the French presence in this Muslim land were close if not identical. It is, one must add, in this context that Eberhardt was as much a part of the colonial scene as Lyautey himself was. A recent and probing article on her unfinished and largely autobiographical, novel Trimadeur (1922)[4] goes so far as to say that although Eberhardt was very much out of tune with the prevailing mood of Algerian colonization, she was nonetheless receptive to the far more sophisticated techniques toward achieving the same ends that Lyautey was to develop in Morocco.[5] This may very well be true, and it seems logical enough. The other issue, which of course gained far more notoriety at the time, of whether or not Isabelle, paper-thin, unattractive, sunken-cheeked, shaven-headed and losing all her teeth, became Lyautey's mistress now seems quite beside the point, which is that the relationship between them was an intellectual student-teacher one.

Hence all the evidence points to the fact that Eberhardt completely swallowed Lyautey's ideas of pénétration pacifique. It would be needlessly harsh today to blame her for having done so, as between

99

this and her outspoken championship of Algerian Islam there is, in terms of the times and the context, no real inconsistency. Lyautey was particularly interested in the fact that Isabelle had become a member of the Qadiriya, and he saw immediately how, as such, she could fit into his plans.

She saw his designs for colonization as being humane in comparison with those currently employed in Algeria; she valued his friendship; and it may even have been possible that she wanted to redeem somewhat her vaguely anti-French reputation and activities. So she became in fact an unofficial agent of the Deuxième Bureau.[6] She was poorly paid, but, although (unlike Picard) she was not out for material benefits, she insisted on a minimum to keep her horse. More important, in her view, was that she had almost complete freedom of the post and was able to follow with the troops, with whom, as always, she was on excellent terms. From 'Ain Sfra down to Beni Ounif and across the Figuig on the Moroccan side of the frontier, she was able to ride the outlying oases with only a single escort, drinking in impressions, most of which she noted down and made sketches to take to Victor Barrucand in Algiers for publication in <u>al-Akhbar</u> or the <u>Dépêche Algérienne</u>.

She did not return to 'Ain Sfra until May 1904, by which time Lyautey had gone down to Bèchar to organize reconnaissance teams to send into the Bni Gil in Moroccan territory. In this endeavor he wanted to enlist the aid of the mrabtin (saints) of Qnadsa who were saints of the Ziyaniya order (an offshoot of the Nasiriya which had been established in its present location around 1733). The first role envisaged for the top shaikh of the order was that of mediator between the Bu' Amama, the Bni Gil, and the Dawi Mani' on the one hand and the French on the other, with the French treated as just another tribe. Not only did this kind of back-and-forth arbitration act as a brake on continued tribal resistance and tend to fragment it, but it seems that Sidi Brahim effectively threw the full weight of his support over to the French. And he was convinced by none other than Isabelle Eberhardt, who, acting on Lyautey's orders, had ridden out to persuade him that this was in his best interests, and in those of the order. He asked for French protection after having been recruited into the Franco-Moroccan Border Commission under General Cauchemez.[7] Sidi Brahim had become a major lever in

French penetration and there seems little doubt that Isabelle had had a hand in making it so.

Her constant ill health combined with the ruthless sun and the sand-laden winds took great toll on Isabelle's looks. Her beautiful black eyes were usually bright with fever, and her teeth had rotted away through near-starvation, kif smoking, and heavy absinthe drinking: she was only twenty-seven but had quite lost what little feminine allure she once had. Despite her mystic fervor and perpetual search for Truth and Oneness with a sublime being, she was unable to find true peace but was torn between the life of the eternal vagabond and that of the recluse. She longed for stability but would have scoffed had this idea been put to her. When under the influence of liquor and kif she sank into reveries of despair. As Isabelle wrote in her diary and as Mackworth poignantly observes: "I am utterly alone, no home, no country, no family. Yes, it really is written that such should be my life."[8]

The terrible climate of Qnadsa, where malaria was rife, devastated Isabelle's already weak health, and she would lie for hours, even days, in a delirium looked after by a Sundanese slave belonging to Sidi Brahim and watched over from afar, by Sidi Brahim's mother who sent tea and food. When Isabelle was well enough to listen, the slave would gossip about her mistress and the household: the black and white women, wives, slaves, concubines; the quarrels, the jealousies, the intrigues. Over all this ruled calmly and supremely Sidi Brahim's mother. She was scrupulous in her hospitality, a pious woman who was feared and venerated by all. She seldom went out and only then, heavily veiled, to visit the tombs of Sidi bin Bu Ziyyan and Sidi Muhammad, her late husband. Isabelle wondered about this woman who she could never meet on account of her false identity. What were the thoughts of this lady, queen-mother almost, cloistered and yet invested with an authority before which even her son bowed?[9] In Sidi Brahim's house, Isabelle was sheltered and cared for because no matter how destitute a person in a Muslim country might be, he is rarely left to suffer or die alone. Someone always shares his own meager crust, if necessary, the devout believing that their compassion will be rewarded in Paradise. But Isabelle's strong character came to the fore. She rebelled against her poor health and the fever left her for a while. It was then that her host, Sidi Brahim, asked if she would mind sharing her room with two visitors. To all intents she was a young man, a <u>talib</u> in search of truth and learning. One was a young man from the Ait 'Atta, quick to avenge his family and friends and therefore nicknamed "the man of powder" as he spoke with his gun. He was accompanied by his black protege, Mulay Sahil. They had been sent as envoys by the shaikh of the Ziyaniya earlier. These two had taken part in the raid and now begged Sidi Brahim's forgiveness which he granted, being a kind old man. During their short stay the three of them became friends, as Sidi Brahim knew they would, and, now that Isabelle was better, he urged her to travel west with them. It was a polite and tactful way of indicating that it was time to move on; fever-ridden Isabelle must have been a worry to the family. The journey would take a month through the Tafilalt in southeastern Morocco with vague plans of possibly traveling yet further west into that country. In pressing Eberhardt to push into Morocco, the old shaikh no doubt had his own interests in mind, as he figured her subsequent reports to Lyautey would be in his favor especially since she would have the guidance of his own men. He assured her of her safety: as she would be under the protection of two men from the Ait 'Atta, she would reach her destination unharmed or the men would die with her.

Isabelle dearly wanted to undertake this march, but feared the rigors of such a journey and the fact that she might be a burden to her companions. She decided to go to 'Ain Sfra to the hospital where she could get treatment and by so doing, sealed her fate. Her heart heavy with this necessary decision Isabelle rode out of Qnadsa with her two friends until they came to a lonely cemetery which was the parting of the ways. There, as is customary, they dismounted and kissed one another three times across the right shoulder.

"Go in peace and the keeping of God," said al-Husain.

"And may all be well with you," replied Isabelle. And so saying they mounted and took their respective paths.

Isabelle rode up a hillock and looked back at her two friends; then, with tears in her eyes, she urged her horses to a gallop and headed toward Bechar and 'Ain Sfra.[10]

Though Isabelle was a master of desert trails, the journey was hard and lonely and again she became a victim of her almost constant malaria. When she arrived at 'Ain Sfra, she was almost prostrate with one of the worst bouts she had ever suffered. There was nothing for it except to go into the military hospital and submit to the onerous discipline. The doctors were shocked by her weak and emaciated condition and marveled at the toughness of her spirit which had enabled her to continue to lead such an active and harsh life for so long.

Her thoughts flew to Sliman; though often physically separated, they were together in spirit and constantly wrote to each other. Sliman understood well that in order to hold her he had to leave her free to roam and meditate in solitude. Hospital routine bored her and in her worst feverish fits of depression she felt near to death. She wandered around the hospital courtyard from where she gazed out across the desert and thought about the distant oases that she would visit, and she wrote in her journal her melancholy thoughts: "To die with ecstasy, to experience this last strange mystery; the end of everything or a divine beginning. . . . Death exerts a strange attraction over my imagination."[11]

Isabelle wrote to Sliman begging him to visit her at 'Ain Sfra and, after an agonizing period of time, he was granted leave of absence from his job as caretaker in Setif, and he telegraphed his imminent arrival. Isabelle was overjoyed and infused with a fresh vigor for life. She determined to rent accommodation in the low-lying quarter of the town, ignoring the doctors' protests that she was still not well enough to leave the hospital; she wanted to be with Sliman, they had been parted so long. With him she wanted to while away the nights with absinthe and kif, making love and murmuring poetry, recapturing the earlier days in the moonlit oases gardens.

In the mud-and-straw houses of the village Isabelle found a two-roomed dwelling, one room above the other with an outside staircase and a terrace. She took the top room and here felt at home and at peace, momentarily free of her compulsive urge to wander. She was content with her husband, and the aromatic fumes of kif added the illusion of eternal happiness to their fleeting hours together.

Lethargically, in the calm windless air of early morning, she roused herself to shop for the barest necessities and then hurried back to Sliman. Though Isabelle was unable to stay in any one place for long, theirs must have been a true love match, and Sliman must have been a man of tender insight to see beneath Isabelle's ravaged exterior and so love the sensitive, restless woman within. Briefly, in the coolness of their crumbling abode, she felt loved and utterly tranquil in the faith of Islam. Isabelle, the mystic, never counted on tomorrow. She accepted the fact that death is imminent, yet it will never be known whether she had a presentiment that her own death was so close.

Ironically, just before the flash flood that carried away most of 'Ain Sfra and drowned Isabelle Eberhardt Ahanni, an announcement was published in the Algiers newspaper Le Mobacher on 19 October 1904, that the temperature had dropped considerably although no rain had fallen in the region. As a result, owing to lack of water, the dates had ripened and been harvested too soon, and everyone was anxiously awaiting the first rains in order to start that season's plowing.

Then in the early hours of the morning of October 21, the heavens opened over the hinterland of 'Ain Sfra. The hard-baked earth, unable to absorb a heavy and sudden downpour, let the rain flood through the dry gullies accumulating the whole into a single powerful torrent that swept down through the main riverbed to an unsuspecting village which had not even been spattered by a drop of rain, nor heard a single rumble of thunder.

'Ain Sfra itself was laid out in two parts divided by a deep gorge. Two or three hundred feet above this perched the garrison with its military hospital and officers' quarters, while below, on the opposite side, was the Arab settlement. The gorge was spanned by a bridge, but since the countryside was usually parched, footpaths crisscrossed the riverbed between the village and the garrison above; these were shortcuts between the French and native quarters. Isabelle herself used these paths when she wanted to visit General Lyautey or her Legionnaire friends for a convivial get-together. The following description is by a German legionnaire eye-witness as recorded in his report.

> Towards nine o'clock, the sergeant-major sent me to take a message to the Intendency in town. I hurried and was back in time for breakfast . . . I fetched my mess-tin from the kitchen and was beginning my meal on the corner of the office table, when the quarter-master, who was standing by the open door, called out "Kohn, come and look . . . Quickly! By God the whole

104

village down there is going under the water! And listen to that row!

I joined him immediately . . . a yellow torrent of bubbling water was rushing through the raving _wadi_, between the town and the camp, carrying masses of rubbish, trees, _zaribas_. Now the water was invading the quarters from which I had just returned. Between the town and the redoubt was a sort of river, full of rapids and whirlpools that widened as they swirled down, and all communication was cut off. Suddenly there was a noise of thunder and I saw the bridge collapse.

At that time of day there were very few soldiers in the civilian part of 'Ain Sfra; the bugles had sounded for breakfast and the legionnaires were at their meal. Most of the officers lived at the redoubt and took their meals at the mess. At this very moment we were all assembled in front of the camp and were watching with anguish while the town disappeared beneath the flood. We asked ourselves how we could help the inhabitants. One of our comrades, a soldier from Lorraine, named Beck, noticed the postman, his wife and little child clinging to the roof of their house, in imminent danger of death. Beck was a fine chap and tried to assist the poor wretches. He threw himself into the water, but could not overcome the current. He had just risen from his meal and must have been seized by cramp as we saw him carried away, rolled over and over by the current to disappear before our eyes. Meanwhile, the roof on which the postman and his family had taken refuge, and where they were screaming for help, collapsed into the rushing water and the poor things were carried away in their turn. At this moment the whole of the lower part of the native town was under water.

It was not till four in the afternoon that some of my comrades and I managed to throw a strong rope across the torrent, where other rescuers had attached it firmly. When this was done

105

we tried to cross the river, which was beginning to go down, by clinging to the rope. Our efforts were all in vain, the water was freezing cold and it was impossible to remain in it for long. Lyautey sent us the order to desist, since our enterprise, as he said himself, was beyond human strength. It was not till late in the night that we managed to improvise a bridge by the light of our lanterns, utilizing ammunition wagons, carts and <u>arabas</u>. The water was receding rapidly and the current diminishing.[12]

After Isabelle's death this same legionnaire, Richard Kohn, wrote to Robert Randau, her old friend, with his personal comments about the woman they all considered their friend.

You can imagine how we crowded around her as soon as she arrived in the canteen. Our ignorance of the French language cut us off from the outside world and the legionnaires have been on pretty bad terms with the civilians of Sidi-bel-Abbès [where Isabelle had spent some time previously, and where Aurélie had a sister living], where we had recently been stationed. We really took a keen pleasure in talking our own language to a person who spoke it with such elegance. It reminded us of home.

She took an interest in our private lives, told us her brother had been in the Legion and questioned us on our reasons for joining it. Then she told us a whole lot of stories, especially about her wanderings in the <u>bled</u> [the countryside, the 'sticks'].

Between ourselves, I must tell you that we were secretly flattered that she preferred the company of us soldiers to that of the officers. We knew that she was a friend of our chief, Lyautey; I had seen her one day sitting opposite him by a desk in the room at which he used to write his reports and where I had come to install the electricity (I used to be an electrician by profession). They were whispering, leaning toward each other.

But it is my duty to tell you that none of us ever thought of flirting with her. Sometimes ten or twelve of us would stay gossiping with her, but none of my comrades, any more than myself, would have permitted himself the slightest bad language in her presence. Moreover, she was not in the least flirtatious, nor at all pretty. Various people who knew her have spoken of her indecent conduct, but none of the legionnaires she frequented at 'Ain Sfra would have agreed with them. There are some who pretend that she was the mistress of Lyautey, either when he was a colonel or when he was given the rank of general. That is a pure calumny, for my mates and I often used to meet our chief in the evening, returning to the fort with girls from the dance hall whom he brought home with him.[13]

Lyautey, as well as the officers of the garrison and hospital knew that Isabelle had rented a mud-and-straw _gurbi_ (hut) in the Arab village in order to be with Sliman, yet they were helpless as they watched the village below being swept away. Lyautey was frantic in his concern for Isabelle and ordered one of his officers, Lieutenant de Loustel, to leave no stone unturned toward her recovery; her fate was already a foregone conclusion. Lyautey, with his intimate knowledge of Isabelle's negative outlook and firm belief in destiny, _qisma_, or _maktub_, suspected that she would have made no effort to save herself. In fact she might have welcomed this sudden death as a solution to her own unhappy problems and the misery of her life.

Sliman had survived the flood and was taken to de Loustel's office utterly distraught. He gave a babbled and almost incoherent account to the lieutenant of what had happened. He was all the more bemused, for throughout the terrifying experience not a drop of rain had fallen; in fact the sky had been clear. He described to the officer what he thought had happened:

We were on the balcony of our room on the first floor. All of a sudden we heard a grumbling sound that seemed like a procession of lorries advancing. The noise grew louder and louder. People passed by, running; they cried out "l-wad! l-wad!" The river! The river! I did not understand. The weather was clear and there was neither rain nor storm. A great mass of water arrived in the bed of the ravine in an instant; it rose up like a wall; it ran like a galloping horse; it was at least two meters high; it was carrying trees and furniture, bodies of animals and men.

I saw the danger and we fled. The torrent caught us up. I do not know how I escaped. My wife was carried away.[14]

Once the flood waters had diminished, the riverbed was a chaos of wreckage, corpses and animals many of which had been swept for miles downstream in the raging water. There was no sign of Isabelle; yet Lyautey, in his mounting anxiety, insisted that the search continue yet further afield, but it was to no avail. If Isabelle had been carried away in the river she would almost certainly have been found. Finally, despite Sliman's account and after days of looking, the commandant ordered that a search be made of the house itself. Again, de Loustel was in charge of this grisly operation.

The house stood at a corner of an alley and was the only one to have been destroyed at that point. The stench of death and decay was everywhere, but as the soldiers approached the ruins a more suffocating odor assailed them and they knew what they could expect to find. Grimly they tore away great slabs of plaster, rafters and boulders, and there, pinned beneath a beam, the body of Isabelle was exposed. As though in prayer her legs were doubled beneath her and her hands locked behind her neck, in, possibly, an instinctive reflex at self-preservation. To Lyautey and everyone else, it remained a mystery why Isabelle drowned when she was fleeing to safety, while her husband survived the wall of water that came tumbling down.

She had always felt she would like to die young, and, according to Mme Arnaud (Mme Randau), who was already in her late nineties when she agreed to see the present author in November 1976, Isabelle sometimes talked of strange visions she had had when she rode alone in the desert of a Russian ancestor, and she was convinced that it was a warning of her own approaching death.

Perhaps, after the first horrifying sight of the water rushing toward her, she gave herself up to her vision and turned back as they raced down the outside staircase. Here, at last was the end to her tormented and unfulfilled life. The great mystery that had so often haunted her was about to be solved.

Isabelle's funeral was simple, as she would have wished; she was carried on an open bier in Muslim style to the local cemetery. Lyautey himself chose her headstone--a plain basalt slab understandingly and compassionately labeled "Lalla Mahmuda" (feminine version of 'Si Mahmud') with a verse from the Qur'an chiseled into it and a smaller, plain slab at her feet. This marked her out as a noteworthy person in a land where simple people have no more than two completely unmarked stones to show where they lie.

Unlike Aurélie Picard, there was no question that Isabelle lived and died a Muslim. The thirst for absolute truth dragged her toward love affairs, kif and absinthe. Aurélie, on the other hand, was destined to command men, build houses and be buried beside the mausoleum of her husband, Sidi Ahmad. [15]

Despite Lyautey's protection, the memory of Isabelle Eberhardt was one of reprobation, as it had been in her lifetime. She seemed to be remembered only for her sexual excesses and drinking debaucheries, not, of course among her co-religionists but among, in particular, the ladies of the colonial establishment who considered themselves so worthy and above reproach. If they had ever had any dreams or desires to be different, they certainly never had the courage to carry them out in the face of outrage and opposition as Isabelle had done.

If fate had not taken pity on her and freed her when it did, she might well have lived to see Algeria gain its independence and possibly even to have fought alongside her Muslim brothers to expel the foreign, infidel invaders.

CONCLUSION

Aurélie Picard and Isabelle Eberhardt--one is struck by the obvious differences between them in background, social class, education and outlook. The first was a highly conventional Frenchwoman of the lower petite bourgeoisie; the second an unconventional Russian near-aristocrat. But one is also struck and more deeply, by the fact that whatever the means and the motives, they were both drawn to Islam as manifested in Colonial Algeria of the late nineteenth century. Their unique opportunities for contact with Algerian Muslims as individuals and with Algerian Muslim society in the northern Sahara in general--whether at the level of the leading shaikh of a prestigious though collaborationist religious order or at that of humble Algerian spahi in the French colonial army-- render these two women subjects worthy of study.

Seen in this wider context, it no longer seems to matter so much that Picard was consentingly and overtly a tool of the French colonial establishment while Eberhardt, despite her objections to the system, was its more unwitting servant and possibly even a kind of Algerian protonationalist. Whether it is indeed accurate to label Picard's conduct reprehensible and Eberhardt's courageous but irresponsible, the two women do complement each other. Both have places in the wide landscape of colonizers and colonized, and it is their contribution to the whole canvas of the French colonial scene as much as their intrinsic interest which makes the stories of Picard and Eberhardt worthy of presenting to a wider public.

CONCLUSION

Aurélie Picard and Isabelle Eberhardt—one is struck by the obvious differences between them in background, social class, education and outlook. The first was a highly conventional Frenchwoman of the lower petite bourgeoisie, the second an unconventional Russian near-aristocrat. But one is also struck and more deeply, by the fact that whatever the means and the motives, they were both drawn to Islam as manifested in Colonial Algeria of the late nineteenth century. Their unique opportunities for contact with Algerian Muslims as individuals and with Algerian Muslim society in the northern Sahara in general—whether at the level of the leading shaikh of a prestigious though collaborationist religious order or at that of humble Algerian spahi in the French colonial army—render these two women subjects worthy of study.

Seen in this wider context, it no longer seems to matter so much that Picard was consentingly and overtly a tool of the French colonial establishment while Eberhardt, despite her objections to the system, was its more unwitting servant and possibly even a kind of Algerian protonationalist. Whether it is indeed accurate to label Picard's conduct reprehensible and Eberhardt's courageous but irresponsible, the two women do complement each other. Both have places in the wide landscape of colonizers and colonized, and it is their contribution to the whole canvas of the French colonial scene as much as their intrinsic interest which makes the stories of Picard and Eberhardt worthy of presenting to a wider public.

APPENDICES

Appendix A

DOCTRINE AND TEACHINGS OF THE TIJANIYA ORDER

The following is an account of the doctrine and teachings of the Tijaniya Order as laid down by its founder, Sidi Ahmad al-Tijani the Elder, after his vision at Sidi Bu Simghun.

According to Arabic documents on the Tijaniya, Sidi Ahmad al-Tijani the Elder-Founder claimed to have two saintly positions at once, that of the "pole of the poles" (qutb al-aqtab) and that of "seal of Muhammadan sainthood" (khatm al-wilaya al-muhammadiya). Among the various ascriptions of the former were impeccability and infallibility which Sidi Ahmad the Founder duly claimed for it and hence indirectly for himself. This claim had long caused considerable controversy, and it was not lightly attributed even to prophets, while mere saints were adamantly refused it. Even so, this did not prevent Sidi Ahmad from pushing his claim. In addition, and contrary to the usual practice among Sufi orders, Ahmad al-Tijani evidently left no genealogical or spiritual claim of ascent and authority linking him on a step-by-step basis with the Prophet. Rather, he circumvented this particular hurdle by producing a single one-link silsila which went directly from him to the Prophet.

This claim, as Abun-Nasr notes, was out of tune with the beliefs of other Muslims and hence unacceptable to them—though in our view this is not a valid reason for trying to break Sidi Ahmad's claim to sharifhood. The nub of the matter may well reside precisely in its ambiguity, in which Sidi Ahmad's descendants and followers said yea and neighboring, non-Tijaniya Muslims said nay to these claims. In view of Sidi Ahmad's categorical statements about his personal superiority to all other walis (saints) and the superiority of his tariqa to other Sufi orders, it is not surprising that his claims were disputed. Especially objectionable, no doubt, was the claim that anyone who defected from the Tijaniya order would die an

115

infidel.[1]

In addition, Tijanis were prohibited by the
founder of the order from visiting other living
saints or the shrines of dead ones who were
affiliated with any other tariqa. Given the
importance attached in North African Islam to the
ziyara or pilgrimage to local saints' tombs, a
prohibition of this kind must have caused much
consternation there and in West Africa as well.

Finally, Tijanis must perform three rites in
addition to all Muslims (the so-called five pillars:
profession of faith, prayer five times a day,
compulsory almsgiving, fasting during the month of
Ramadan, and the pilgrimage to Mecca). These three
additional obligations are daily recitation once
after the dawn prayer and once after the evening
prayer of the litanies (wird) and the office
(wazifa) of the order, and participation in the
hadra, or special devotional which accompanies the
noon prayer on Fridays, which to Muslims everywhere
is the main prayer of the week and which is always
performed in the congregational mosque. The details
of the litany need not concern us: every Sufi order
shows slight variations in emphasis, and no two are
exactly alike. One further point of difference with
other orders may however be noted.

Sidi Ahmad claimed to have had the Prophet's
authority that a single recitation of the special
Tijani prayer, the Salat al-Fatih, was equivalent to
the recitation of all other prayers of glorification
to God ever said in the universe as well as to the
recitation of the whole Qur'an six thousand times.
This of course was and is regarded as preposterous
by other Muslims though it certainly serves to set
the Tijaniya apart, both in their own eyes and in
those of others--not always to their credit.[2] The
French explorer Duveyrier maintained that the
friendly attitude of the Tijaniya order to the
French arose because of a belief expressed in the
Salat al-Fatih in which the Prophet is designated as
"he who makes the Truth victorious by Truth." The
first Truth, Duveyrier said, referred to the religion of Islam and the second to God, and he inter-
preted the whole to mean that God was able to ensure
the victory of Islam without the agency of His
creatures. From this he deduced that from this
prayer that the Tijaniya drew the belief--one at
very considerable variance from orthodox Muslim
belief in North Africa and elsewhere--that Muslims
do not in fact need to fight for Islam, since God
could grant victory to the Muslims if He wished.

116

Duveyrier considered this belief the basis of an _entente_ or at least an acceptable modus vivendi between Muslims and Christians.[3] Ahmad Tijani himself, however, explained the Salat al-Fatih as follows: the first Truth did indeed mean the religion of Islam, but the second referred to the ways and means in which it spread, through declaration of its truth without any additions or alterations.[4] Whether the chiefs of the Tijaniya order in nineteenth-century Algeria were motivated by these views is open to question.

An additional factor which would help to explain the attitude of the Algerian Tijaniya is that Muhammad al-Saghir, son of Sidi Ahmad al-Tijani and his successor in 1844-53 as head of the order, believed in avoiding bloodshed at all costs. His ambition to create a state rather than any inherent pacifism underlay Muhammad al-Saghir's relations with both Amir 'Abd al-Qadir and the French since he realized that cooperation was a more effective strategy.

The Tijanis of 'Ain Madi had contested the authority of the Amir 'Abd al-Qadir ever since his election as sultan (of the Algerian rural resistance) by most of the Oranis and the Algerois and thus they were virtually at the head of his list for punishment. There were several reasons why the Tijanis at 'Ain Madi refused to join him against the French: one was because his cause had become identified with a rival Sufi order, the Qadiriya, for it was held in Algeria at the time that the founder of this order, Sidi 'Abd al-Qadir al-Jilali, who was also the Amir's namesake and patron saint, had been responsible for his election as sultan. Another and possibly more basic reason is that 'Abd al-Qadir's own tribe the Bani Hashim had been largely responsible for the betrayal and death in 1827 of Sidi Muhammad al-Kabir al-Tijani. The latter was captured alive by the Turks in battle at Mu'askar (Mascara) and subsequently executed, with his head sent to the Bey of Algiers.

Hence after the 1837 Treaty of the Tafna with the French, which gave 'Abd al-Qadir time to lick his wounds, he turned to the task of subjugating his Muslim opponents in Algeria. In the pursuit of this objective he attacked 'Ain Madi in the summer of 1838. The pretext for the attack was that the Tijanis and the Gharaba or Western tribes of Laghouat who supported them refused to acknowledge the authority of 'Abd al-Qadir's appointed lieutenant over the Sharaga or Eastern tribes of the same region. There is no doubt that the Tijaniya resisted the Amir with all they had and gave him an excellent run for his money, despite his superior manpower. The seige lasted for five months: when 'Abd al-Qadir first attacked he had 3,600 men and two pieces of artillery, and during the siege his reinforcements came to as many as 8,000--this as opposed to 700 on the defenders' side. 'Abd al-Qadir's forces tried several times to storm the walls, but failed, as the Tijanis were able to rebuild at night what had been destroyed by day. He could not starve them out either, as the village was well provisioned. Nevertheless, after a long siege both parties were ready to compromise and an arrangement was reached between Sidi Muhammad al-Saghir al-Tijani and 'Abd al-Qadir's brother-in-law on 17 November 1838, to conclude the siege if the following conditions were met: Sidi Muhammad al-Saghir was to pay the expenses incurred by 'Abd al-Qadir over the past five months, and 'Ain Madi was to be completely evacuated within forty days. In return, the Tijani leader was allowed to take all his movable property with him, the villagers were allowed to join him, and "Abd al-Qadir retired to a safe distance while the evacuation took place with Sidi al-Muhammad al-Saghir's son in his hands as a hostage.

Under these conditions the siege was lifted on 2 December 1838, and the Tijani leader left the village a month later to settle with the Gharaba in Laghouat. Once the evacuation was completed, 'Abd al-Qadir returned to raze the fortifications and destroy the main building and the shaikh's house, which, however, Sidi Muhammad al-Saghir was to rebuild when he returned in November 1840.

If anything, Sidi Muhammad al-Saghir al-Tijani gained somewhat from this encounter, as not only did 'Abd al-Qadir fail to force him to submit publicly, but the protracted length of the seige was in itself deleterious to the Amir's prestige. The Gharaba tribes refused to pay him tribute on the strength of this, and he massacred a number of their men in consequence. The French, however, waiting in the sidelines, were the real gainers, for while 'Abd al-Qadir besieged 'Ain Madi, Marshal Valée reinforced the French army positions in Eastern Algeria and prepared to resume the war which was to end only in 1847 with the Amir's surrender.[5]

Notes

1. Abun-Nasr, <u>The Tijaniya</u>, p. 23.

2. Ibid., p. 51.

3. Ibid., p. 59.

4. Ibid., p. 59.

5. Paraphrased from Ibid., pp. 58-68.

Appendix B

THE RIFT BETWEEN 'AIN MADI AND TAMALHAT AFTER 1898

The long-standing rift between 'Ain Madi and
Tamalhat (mentioned in chapters four and five) now
came fully out into the open after 1898, more so
than it had even been before. The major point of
friction, sparked off by al-Bashir, was his insistence on an issue of exclusivity. Backed with
dogged tenacity by Aurélie Tijani, he held only that
members of the 'Ain Madi branch of the Tijaniya
order be allowed to attach the patronymic
'al-Tijani' to their names. He claimed that the
Tamasin/Tamalhat and Gaymar branches, those
descended from Sidi al-Hajj 'Ali, had no such right
as they were simply muqaddamin of the order. The
members of the Moroccan zawiya in Fez and the other
muqaddamin of the order did not bear the patronymic,
he held; and he added that the Tamalhat members,
whose legitimacy to the same patronymic he contested, should add the qualification al-Tijani
tariqa, "Tijani as a religious order," or that of
al-Tijani shurban/mushraban, "Tijani as a young
spring nourishing (the spirit)." Indeed, Sidi al-
Bashir insisted on the solicitation of higher
authority to push his claim, as is made abundantly
clear in the archives.[1] Even though Louis Lepine,
the Governor-General, to whose attention the matter
came, hoped that it would soon be settled in the
interests of the Tijaniya order at large, the
archives reveal a large file of acrimonious
correspondence, in which French generals in the
Algiers and Constantine Divisions ended up opposing
each other because each group was backing rival
candidates.[2]
Although it seems today to be much ado about
nothing, some of this correspondence is not entirely
without interest, for the simple reason that the
real point of the exercise was not at all which side
was right but rather which side could come one-up on
the other in a stationary power struggle at a distance and by remote control. The evidence is not

necessarily presented in chronological order but rather as points of debate. For example, a letter from Sidi Muhammad al-'Arusi to Tamalhat dated 20 Rajab 1316 (4 December 1896), to the French captain at Tuggurt has it that Sidi al-Bashir's sole object in arrogating the exclusivity of the Tijani patronym to himself was so that he could collect more <u>ziyara</u> offerings.[3] However, once Sidi al-Bashir initiated the matter, a number of French generals were quick either to come to his defense or to attack him and Picard. It is interesting that the defense was continued in the department at Algiers while the attack was concentrated in that of Constantine: in other words, each departmental side was defending its own Tijani constituents. Prominent among the defenders were General Ruyssen (General Commandant Subdivision Laghouat) and General Collet-Meygret (General Commandant Division Algiers), while the major proponent of attack was the adroit General Dechizelle (Commandant Subdivision Batna, in the Constantinois) who was outspoken about his dislike for Picard.[4]

General Collet-Meygret (citing Ruyssen) noted that although Sidi Muhammad al-'Arusi at Gaymar (the nephew of Sidi Muhammad bin Sidi Muhammad al-'Aid, or "Si Hamma") affected airs of independence from 'Ain Madi, he was reported to have kissed the shoulder of Sidi al-Bashir when the latter came to visit. Collet-Meygret also noted that as of April 1898, Sidi al-'Arusi had received no formal investiture and that the residence at Gaymar was not a recognized <u>zawiya</u> but a mere summer resort for the muqaddamin of Tamalhat. He further asserted that Sidi al-'Arusi had created the fuss merely in order to retain the mortal remains of Sidi Ahmad.

General Ruyssen now stepped in supporting Sidi al-Bashir by noting that if at the time of their internment in Algiers the Tijani brothers of 'Ain Madi had had to turn over the running of the affairs of the order to the Tamalhat, they had by no means renounced their birthright in so doing and if they had not up to this time protested the fact that the Tamalhat saints continued to call themselves "al-Tijani" it was because until very recently the latter had always shown themselves to be respectful and loyal servitors of the main lodge. But, he said, this attitude had changed, which was why Sidi al-Bashir was protesting the usurpation of authority arising from the addition of the patronymic to the lineage of someone who was only a muqaddam, and he said that this stricture applied notably to Sidi

al-'Arusi, and "ambitious intriguer" who was not
even that. Ruyssen noted further that such an
attitude could only be prejudicial, as the mother
zawiya had become fortified since Mme Aurélie took
over the direction of its material affairs and since
the intelligent and influential individuals who
acted as counsellors to Sidi al-Bashir concurred in
its spiritual direction.[5] Finally, he stated that a
serious intervention by the authorities would
suffice to keep the Awlad Sidi al-Hajj 'Ali at
Tamalhat and Gaymar from abusing a name which was
not theirs and that the "leadership of the order
should be maintained in the hands of its real
master, who is totally devoted to French interests.[6]

For his part, General Pédoya took a somewhat
different tack by invoking the ambitions of the
Tijaniya order in West Africa and noting that since
the 'Ain Madi saints had been held in Algiers as
political detainees, its progress in the former area
had been slowed down considerably. He added that
once the two brothers from 'Ain Madi came back home
to recuperate their hereditary rights, they reacted
against this. And here he retreats into verbiage,
trying to show that the term "branch" to designate
the zawiyas of Tamasin/Tamalhat and Fez is improper,
as they were mere "succursales" of 'Ain Madi-cum-
Qurdan, as were all other Tijaniya houses, a sort of
emanation of its powers and influence. Pédoya even
refers to his interview with a top Tijani from Wadai
named Yusuf bin Basha who had come due north to see
the late 'Ain Madi incumbent, saying that in his
region everyone had referred to the latter as
"Sidna"--our lord--Ahmad Tijani.[7]

Insofar as we have been able to piece it
together the above seems a representative sampling
of the views of the 'Ain Madi supporters. But they
had to contend with a mind both more vigorous and
more devious than their own, in General Déchizelle
who came out with the full force of his considerable
histrionic and epistolary skills in favor of Sidi
Muhammad al-'Arusi at the Tamalhat/Gaymar zawiyas.
Déchizelle, first of all, considered the rights of
both Sidi Muhammad b. Sidi Muhammad al-'Aid and Sidi
Muhammad al-'Arusi at Gaymar to bear the patronymic
"al-Tijani" to be absolute and undisputed, for their
common ancestor Sidi al-Hajj 'Ali had borne it, as
had his fourteen sons. He noted, further, that one
of the Tamalhat saints had recently spent eight
months at 'Ain Madi and that, during this time, Sidi
al-Bashir had evidently never brought up the matter
of the patronymic, while adding more vaguely that

123

Sidi al-'Arusi had documents showing that the founder of the order, Sidi Ahmad al-Tijani the Elder, had conferred this right on the muqaddam of each of the two lineages.[8]

In an earlier and more revealing letter, Déchizelle reports that Sidi al-'Arusi was not surprised to hear that Sidi al-Bashir's claim to be the sole individual with the right to bear the "al-Tijani" patronymic was dictated by Mme Aurélie, who in his eyes was only the concubine of the late Sidi Ahmad al-Tijani. Sidi al-'Arusi, Déchizelle observed, did not want to talk about the lack of morality and scruples of Sidi al-Bashir and Mme Aurélie, who in his opinion wanted to undertake a vexation campaign against the Tijaniya of Tamalhat whose loyalty to France, once again, had never been questioned. Sidi al-'Arusi regarded the present (or coming) union of Sidi al-Bashir with Mme Aurélie as difficult to excuse, since it was between a French-woman and a non-naturalized Muslim (in effect, Gueydon's earlier argument against her first mar-riage with Sidi Ahmad). Still more "scandalous," in Déchizelle's opinion, was the conduct of these two individuals toward the benefactors of Sidi Ahmad. He argued that neither the Tamalhat nor the Gaymar branches should abandon the patronymic and that "the best way to avoid a scandal would be to invite Mme Aurélie and then Sidi Al-Bashir to abandon their pretensions which are in any case without any serious basis in fact." This last is questionable in the light of later research.[9] He goes on to state that Sidi al-'Arusi considered Mme Aurélie a trouble-making adventuress and that the ever-increasing popularity of Sidi al-'Arusi since Sidi Ahmad's death seemed to be casting a shadow on Sidi al-Bashir and Mme Aurélie, both of whom were ready to go to any lengths to regain the prestige of the 'Ain Madi lodge. And he concludes, eloquently:

> The name "Tijani" is a generic one applying not only to the descendants of the master Sidi Ahmad al-Tijani (the Elder) but also to all his religious servitors: it is indeed the name of the order; and one considers that here is no usurpation on the part of Sidi al-'Arusi in adding the patronymic in ques-tion to his name. I hope that, despite the opinion of Comdt. Pujat [who must have been in the 'Ain Madi camp and whose opinions were evidently contrary

to Déchizelle's], higher authority will help to iron out these dissensions and rivalries between the two branches of "our" Tijaniya which are as prejudicial to our own interests as they are to the order itself.[10]

Although after this point the voluminous correspondence on the issue dries up, there is every reason to believe that the issue subsided with time; certainly it was never resolved. A storm in a teapot, indeed, and possibly also an indication that the upper echelons of military administration in Colonial Algeria at the turn of the century may not have had much to occupy their time.

Sidi Ahmad had always hoped to secure support from the French administration through the influence of his French wife in order to gain authority over his rivals. In this he was not entirely successful. The fact is that the French considered the _zawiya_ of Tamalhat more useful in serving their interests in Tunisia, since it was quite close to the Tunisian border and had closer links with the transborder _zawiyas_. Sidi Ahmad was keenly aware of this, and the archives are full of correspondence relating to his constantly repeated attempts to go to Tunisia-- especially after the implantation of the French protectorate there in 1881--on _ziyara_-collecting expeditions. These effects were all thwarted by the administration. Sidi Ahmad himself, therefore, never made it to Tunisia, although his brother Sidi al-Bashir had been allowed a token visit there in 1879. On the other hand, the services rendered to the French in Tunisia after the 1864 uprising by the shaikhs of the Tamalhat and Gaymar _zawiyas_ were appreciated to the extent that as of January 1892 they began to receive comfortable annual subsidies, starting at 5,000 piasters. Evidence shows that subsidies of 3,000 francs each were still being paid in 1916.[11]

Even so, Sidi Ahmad believed that personal contacts between his own 'Ain Madi lineage and that of Sidi 'Ali at Tamalhat might help him to push through the claim to be the supreme head of the order. To this end he sent his brother Sidi al-Bashir to Tamalhat in 1884. But this visit and subsequent reciprocal orders by the Tijaniya leaders of the Suf region to the 'Ain Madi _zawiya_, resulted only in an exchange of gifts and did not convince the Tamalhat shaikhs of Sidi Ahmad's spiritual leadership and authority.

Notes

1. For example, AGGA, Series H, Box 16 H 57, Dossier No. 7 bis: GGA to Gen. Com. Div. Constantine, June 28, 1899, with a fuller account in AGGA, Series H, Box 16 H 63, GGA, Minute de la lettre Ecrite, Algiers Nov. 30, 1898.

2. As of Rabi' 1-Awwal 1317 or July 17, 1899 (GGA Minute de la lettre Ecrite, Algiers, Nov. 30, 1898).

3. AGGA, Series H, Box 16 H 57, Dossier No. 7 bis. GGA to Gen. Com. Div. Constantine, June 28, 1899.

4. See, for example, AGGA, Series H, Box 16 H 63, Esp. Gen. Ruyssen, Com. Subdiv. Laghouat, to Gen. Collet-Meygret, Com. Div. Algiers, No. 47, Nov. 28, 1898; Gen. Collet-Meygret, Com. Div. Algiers, to GGA, No. 111, Sept. 3, 1896; May 1, 1897; and April 25, 1898; Lt. Falconetti to Capt. Bureau Arabe Laghouat, April 28, 1897; and Gen. Pedoya, Com. Div. Algiers (who may have replaced Collet-Meygret?), to GGA, May 14, 1899. But see also Gen. Déchizelle, Com. Subdiv. Batna, to Gen. Com. Div. Constantine, No. 1627, July 27, 1899; and, in more detail, Déchizelle to Gen. Com. Div. Constantine, April 15,, 1899, and in Box 16 H 57, Dossier No. 7 bis. Déchizelle to Gen. Com. Div. Constantine, March 9, 1900.

5. This approval of Aurélie Picard's running of the zawiya affairs at Qurdan, at the request of al-Bashir, is also enthusiastically taken up by Gen. Collet-Meygret as early as ten days after Sidi Ahmad's death. Cf. AGGA, Series H, Box 16 H 63, Gen. Collet-Meygret, Gen. Com. Div. Algiers to GGA, May 1, 1897.

6. AGGA, Series H, Box 16 H 63, Gen. Ruyssen, Gen. Com. Subdiv. Laghouat, to Gen. Collet-Meygret, Gen. Div. Algiers, No. 147, Nov. 28, 1898.

7. AGGA, Series H, Box 16 H 63, Gen. Pédoya, Com. Div. Algiers, to GGA, May 14, 1899.

8. AGGA, Series H, Box 16 H 53, Gen. Déchizelle,

Com. Subdiv. Batna, to Gen. Com. Div. Constantine, July 27, 1899.

9. AGGA, Series H, Box 16 H 53, Gen. Déchizelle to Gen. Com. Div. Constantine, Dec. 20, 1898.

10. Ibid.

11. Abun-Nasr, <u>The Tijaniya</u>, pp. 79-80.

Appendix C

SUMMARY OF THE QADIRIYA ORDER

It was during the fifteenth century that the Qadiriya order rose in popularity, and what is remarkable about this particular order is both its spread and its depth throughout the world of Islam, encompassing an infinitely wider radius than the Tijaniya. The latter are a localized order restricted to Northwest and West Africa, while the former are found from Morocco to Pakistan. The founder-ancestor of the Qadiriya Order, 'Abdal-Qadir al-Jilani (1077-1166), an Iranian from Gilan on the Caspian shore who is buried in Baghdad, was to become--possibly even during his lifetime--a universalistic and pan-Islamic figure. Shrines commemorating him, literally abound all over the Muslim world, even in places such as Morocco which he certainly never visited. Everywhere he went he was renowned for his sermons and religious instruction. Trimingham has rightly noted that it is difficult to discern just why 'Abd al-Qadir al-Jilani, out of the hundreds of saintly figures of his day, should have been singled out for such very posthumous treatment, but there is no question but that he was so singled out. As a strictly orthodox Hanbali (from which rite the Wahhabis of Saudi Arabia were later to develop), he himself would probably have been repelled at the cultism and veneration that still surrounds him, especially in view of the fact that the Qadiriya variant of Sufism shows no significant departure from predecessor or contemporary orders.[1] The order simply "caught on," and 'Abdal-Qadir al-Jilani is regarded by the faithful as a receiver of petitions and a bestower of benefits to this day.

Notes

1.   J.S. Trimingham, The Sufi Orders of Islam, Oxford: Clarendon Press, 1971, pp. 40-4.

129

NOTES

Chapter 1

1. Cf. William Spencer. <u>Algiers in the Age of the Corsairs</u>. Center of Civilization Series, Norman: University of Oklahoma Press, 1976.

2. Jamil Abun-Nasr. <u>The Tijaniya: A Sufi Order in the Modern World</u>. London: Oxford University Press, 1965, p. 16. Abun-Nasr says only that there is no evidence for any of Sidi Ahmad's ancestors in the patriline having claimed to be a sharif.

3. As both Ernest Gellner and David M. Hart have observed in two additional but similar Moroccan contexts, here "Vox Dei" and "Vox Populi," the Voice of God and the Voice of the People, are identical. Cf. Ernest Gellner, "Concepts and Society," <u>Transactions of the Fifth World Congress of Sociology</u>, Washington, D.C., vol. I, 1962, pp. 153-183; and David M. Hart, <u>The Aith Waryaghar of the Moroccan Rif</u>, Viking Fund Publications in Anthropology No. 55, Tucson: University of Arizona Press, 1976, pp. 256-60.

4. Abun-Nasr, <u>The Tijaniya</u>, 1965, p. 23.

5. Paul Azan, <u>Conquête et Pacification de l'Algérie</u>, Paris, 1931, pp. 385-6. Cited by Abun-Nasr, <u>The Tijaniya</u>, 1965, p. 73.

6. Abun-Nasr, <u>The Tijaniya</u>, p. 74.

7. Ibid., pp. 13-14.

Chapter 2

1. Le Mobacher, no. 141, Archives de Gouvernement Général de l'Algérie (from here on referred to as AGGA), Files ADM, Aix-en-Provence.

Chapter 3

1. Authorization could be found in the Archives des Territoires du Sud du Gouvernement Général de l'Algérie, Carton 164; or the fact was so noted by Elise Crosnier, Aurélie Picard, 1849-1933: Première Française au Sahara, Algiers: Baconnier, 1947, p. 51.

2. Marthe Bassenne. Aurélie Tedjani, Princesse des Sables. 4th Ed. Paris: Plon, 1925, p. 33. Bassenne was her first biographer. Crosnier, her second, produced a later and somewhat more objective account.

3. Le Mobacher, No. 141, AGGA, ADM, Aix-en-Provence.

4. Bassenne, Aurélie Tedjani, pp. 40-2.

5. Leon Roches. Trente-Deux Ans à Travers de l'Islam, 1832-64. 2 vols., Paris: Firmin Didet, 1884-5.

6. AGGA Series J. Bureaux Arabes de la Div. d'Oran, Box 1 J 174, GGA.

7. AGGA Series H. Box 16 H 56, Tedjani 1850-1888, Gen. Poizat, to GGA, Sept. 24, 1887. Also cited by Crosnier Aurélie Picard, pp. 109-10. It is of further interest to note that in the very same letter Gen. Poizat notes that the Court of Appeal at Algiers had just compelled Sidi Ahmad to repay the sum of 16,000 Frs. to Qaid al-Hajj Zigham of the Awlad Ya'qub ash-Shraga tribe on a loss through theft of flocks which the latter had been steadily claiming from him since 1864, over twenty years earlier. Sidi Ahmad claimed that the theft (which evidently occurred at 'Ain Madi) had happened during his absence and that in any event he could not pay it back as he himself owned nothing, all the property of which he enjoyed the use being part of the habus, the religious endowment, of the zawiya. As the

report notes, this was certainly not the case of the farm at Qurdan. Another letter in the same box, Gen. Wolff, Com. Div. Algiers, to GGA, No. 894, Dec. 19, 1894, refers to an even bigger outstanding debt of 15,000 duros or 75,000 Frs., which Ahmad acknowledged having owed Agha al-Din of Jabal Amur ever since 1963-64, when Rihan was still in charge of zawiya affairs. He had deferred payment, alleging that he had lent the Agha large sums because of a severe drought a year or two later. Yet another letter in the same box from Gen. Collet-Meygret, Com. Div. Algiers, to GGA, No. 64, Jan. 21, 1898, indicated that the matter had not come to a satisfactory conclusion even then and that perhaps Mme Aurelie Tijani could shed some light on it.

8. Emile Dermenghem. Le Pays d'Abel. Paris: Gallinard, 1960, pp. 160, 165.

9. Abun-Nasr, The Tijaniya, pp. 68-9.

Chapter 4

1. Abun-Nasr, The Tijaniya, pp. 101-56, provides an analysis in depth.

2. Bassenne, Aurélie Tedjani, pp. 153-4.

3. Ibid., pp. 154-60.

4. Crosnier, Aurélie Picard, p. 121.

5. Ibid., pp. 90-4.

6. Ibid., p 162.

7. AGGA, Series H, Box 16 H 63, Gen. Collet-Meygret to Governor General of Algeria (gga), Jan. 13, 1897.

8. Cf. for example, AGGA, Series H, Box 16 H 63, Gen. Ruyssen, Com. Subdiv. Laghouat, to Gen. Collet-Meygret, Cm. Div. Algiers, No. 47, Nov. 28, 1898; and Gen. Pédoya, Cm. Div. Algiers to GGA May 14, 1899; and before Sidi Ahmad's death, Collet-Meygret to GGA, No. 111, Sept. 3, 1896.

9. Cf. for example his letter (AGGA, Series H, Box 16 H 63) to Comdt. Pujat dated 14 Ramadan 1315 (Feb. 6, 1898), to be passed on to Gen. de la Roque and ultimately to GGA.

10. AGGA Series H, Box 16 H 63, Gen. Déchizelle to Gen. Cm. Subdiv. Constantine, Dec. 20, 1898, Déchizelle vigorously upheld the views of Sidi al-'Arusi.

11. AGGA Series H, Box 16 H 57, Gen. Fontebride, Cm. Subdiv. Batna, to Gen. Cm. Div. Constantine, Jan. 29, 1898.

Chapter 5

1. This approval of Aurélie Picard's running the zawiya affairs at Qurdan at the request of al-Bashir is enthusiastically taken up by Gen. Collet-Meygret as early as ten days after Sidi Ahmad's death. Cf. AGGA Series H, Box 16 H 63. Gen. Collet-Meygret, Gen. Com. Div. Algiers to GGA, May 1, 1897.

2. Bassenne, Aurélie Tedjani, pp. 204-5.

3. The account to follow is taken from AGGA Series H, Box 16 H 64, No. 36 bis. C: Minutes: (Proces-Verbal) of the operations which took place in the Tijaniya zawiya following the death of al-Bashir. The declaration in question was signed by Mme Aurélie Picard July 11, 1911.

4. Bassenne, Aurélie Tedjani, p. 221.

Chapter 6

1. He also continued the tradition of extravagant ziyara collections. In 1913 he went into the Constantine province, and, even though the permit expressly stated that it was forbidden to him to collect ziyara, he nonetheless amassed a total of 11,130 Frs. Capt. Martin, Tuggurt, to Com. mil. territory at Biskra, May 10, 1913, AGGA Series H, Box 16 H 63.

2. Crosnier, Aurélie Picard, 1849-1933, pp. 152-6.

3.   Ibid., p. 153.

Chapter 7

1.   Mackworth, <u>The Destiny of Isabelle Eberhardt</u>, 2nd. Ed., New York: Ecco Press, 1975, p. 36.

2.   Ibid., p. 23.

3.   Ibid., p. 36, n. 1.

4.   This is ably brought out by Mackworth, Ibid., pp. 51-2.

Chapter 8

1.   Mackworth, <u>Isabelle Eberhardt</u>, p. 97.

2.   Louis Rinn. <u>Marabouts et Khouan: Études sur l'Islam en Algérie</u>. Algiers: Adolphe Jourdan, 1884, pp. 183-4.   But for a much more modern interpretation, cf. J. Spencer Trimingham, <u>The Sufi Orders in Islam</u>, Oxford: Clarendon Press, 1971.   Unfortunately there is no single study of the Qadiriya of the caliber of Abun-Nasr on the Tijaniya.

3.   Mackworth, <u>Isabelle Eberhardt</u>, pp. 103-4.

4.   Ibid., pp. 114-5.

5.   Ibid., p. 111, footnote 1, Mackworth only gives this interpretation footnote status, whereas we regard it as worthy of elevation to the text.

6.   Ibid., p. 119.

7.   This information was provided by Adjutant-Chef E. Thomine and Jean-Claude Vatin.

Chapter 9

1.   Mackworth, <u>Isabelle Eberhardt</u>, p. 132.

2.   The na'ib in question had been killed in French service while attempting to mediate between the French and dissident tribesmen

(some of them evidently even Ait 'Atta from southeastern Morocco) at the Battle of Timimun earlier the same year. The question comes from Mackworth, <u>Isabelle Eberhardt</u>, pp. 132-3.

3. For a good account of the operations on the Algero-Moroccan border at this time, see Ross E. Dunn, <u>Resistance in the Desert: Moroccan Responses to French Imperialism, 1881-1912,</u> London: Crown Helm and Madison: University of Wisconsin Press, 1977, esp. Chapters 6 and 7.

4. <u>Trimardeur</u>, published in 1922, is an account of the vicissitudes and troubles of a young Russian named Dimitri Orshanov, who is modeled on Isabelle's brother Augustin but is even more of a reflection of Isabelle herself. Almost all of Isabelle Eberhardt's literary production was in fact posthumous, only appearing under the editorship of Victor Barrucand as of 1921-22: <u>Trimardeur</u> was the most nearly complete manuscript recovered after the 'Ain Sfra flood in which she was killed. The present author is not competent to discuss the literary merits of her work, but merely wishes to note that much of Barrucand's editorship may have been adulter-ated. The fact that he put his own name as editor on the front page in print of equal or even larger size than hers, in effect claiming the work as his own, touched off the biggest literary-legal battle between him, Isabelle's former editor, and her friend Robert Randau (also a publicist, who wrote under the name of Arnaud) that Colonial Algeria ever witnessed.

5. J.H. Gourdon, J.R. Henry & F. Henry-Lorcerie. "Isabelle Eberhardt: <u>Trimardeur</u>," in <u>Revue Algeriénne des Sciences Juridiques, Economiques et Politiques</u>, XI, 1, 1974, pp. 185-93.

6. Mackworth, <u>Isabelle Eberhardt</u>, pp. 192-5.

7. Dunn, <u>Resistance in the Desert</u>, p. 191.

8. Mackworth, <u>Isabelle Eberhardt</u>, p. 216.

9. Stephan, <u>Isabelle Eberhardt ou la Révélation du Sahara</u>, Paris: Flammarion, 1930, p. 219.

10.   Ibid., pp. 229-30.

11.   Ibid., p. 130.

12.   Mackworth, <u>Isabelle Eberhardt</u>, pp. 193-4.

13.   Ibid., pp. 193-4.

14.   Ibid., p. 222.

15.   Dermenghem, <u>Le Pays d'Abel</u>, p. 166.

BIBLIOGRAPHY

Unpublished

All unpublished bibliography is derived from AGGA, the Archives du Gouvernement Général de l'Algérie, in the French archives d'Outre-Mer at Aix-en-Provence. Of particular importance, as indicated in the relevant footnotes, are for Aurélie Picard:

AGGA, Series H, Box 16 H 53
                 Box 16 H 56
                 Box 16 H 57
                 Box 16 H 63

AGGA, Series J, Box 1 J 174

and for Isabelle Eberhardt:

AGGA, Le Mobacher, No. 141

Published

ABUN-NASR, Jamil M. The Tijaniya: A Sufi Order in the Modern World. London, New York, Toronto: Oxford University Press, 1965.

AZAN, Paul. Conquête et Pacification de l'Algérie. Paris, 1931.

BASSENNE, Marthe. Aurélie Tedjani, Princesse des Sables. Paris: Plon, 1925.

CROSNIER, Elise. Aurélie Picard, 1849-1933: Premiere Francaise au Sahara. Algiers: Baconnier, 1947.

DERMENGHEM, Emile. Le Pays d'Abel. Paris: Gallimard, 1960.

DUNN, Ross E. Resistance in the Desert: Moroccan
Responses to French Imperialism, 1881-1912.
London: Crown Helm, and Madison: University of
Wisconsin Press, 1977.

GELLNER, Ernest. "Concepts and Society," Trans-
actions of the Fifth World Congress of
Sociology. Washington, D.C., Vol. I, 1962,
pp. 153-183.

GOURDON, Hubert, HENRY, Jean-Robert and HENRY-
LORCERIE, Francoise, "Isabelle Eberhardt:
Trimardeur." Revue Algérienne des Sciences
Juridiques, Economiques et Politiques. XI, 1,
1974, pp. 185-193.

HART, David M. The Aith Waryaghar of the Moroccan
Rif: An Ethnography and History. Viking Fund
Publications in Anthropology No. 55, Tucson:
University of Arizona Press, 1976.

MACKWORTH, Cecily. The Destiny of Isabelle
Eberhardt. 2nd. Ed., New York: Ecco Press,
1975.

RINN, Louis. Marabouts at Khouan: Études sur
l'Islam en Algerie. Algiers: Adolph Jourdan,
1884.

ROCHES, Leon. Trente-Deux Ans à Travers de l'Islam,
1832-64. 2 vols., Paris: Firmin Didet,
1884-5.

RUEDY, John. Land Policy in Colonial Algeria: The
Origins of the Rural Public Domain. Univer-
sity of California Publications in Near
Eastern Studies, No. 10, Berkeley and Los
Angeles: University of California Press, 1967.

SPENCER, William. Algiers in the Age of the
Corsairs. Center of Civilization Series,
Norman: University of Oklahoma Press, 1976.

STEPHAN, Raoul. Isabelle Eberhardt ou la Revélation
du Sahara. Paris: Flammarion, 1930.

TRIMINGHAM, J. Spencer. The Sufi Orders in Islam.
Oxford: Clarendon Press, 1971.